real women cry
(and real men let them)

Embracing our
God-given
gift of tears

Catherine H. Cieciuch DeBenedetto

real women cry
(and real men let them)

Embracing our
God-given
gift of tears

Catherine H. Cieciuch DeBenedetto

This book is not intended as a substitute for professional medical advice. The reader should consult a licensed professional in matters relating to individual health and wellness particularly in regard to any symptoms that may require diagnosis or medical attention.

Edited by Kathleen Brunet Eagan
Cover Concept by Ronald DeBenedetto
Cover Design by John Van Duyne
Finishing Touches by Michael Zedack

Printed in the United States of America

Library of Congress Control Number: 2015919454
ISBN: 978-1-48356-020-5

Where to begin . . .

Perhaps you have somehow stumbled upon this book—your curiosity awakened by the title. Maybe tears have been your lot in recent days, and a book promising to help you understand them is a welcome balm. Perhaps the word *God* in the subtitle was noticeable to you, but your understanding of Him is little more than that of a cosmic beam somewhere out there in the galaxy or a distant deity ready to strike you down because of a twisted desire to dish out pain and suffering. Maybe you don't believe He exists at all. On the chance that any of this may be true of you, *please know that at this moment the True God of the universe—Who cherishes both women and men—desires for you to know the truth concerning Who He is that you may indeed know His awesome and everlasting love.*

God knew from the beginning that we would fail and make mistakes in our everyday lives. *It came as no surprise to Him that there would be lots of tears.* And while it was always

God's plan for us to be in an intimate relationship with Him (that is why He created us), *any and all form of sin separates us from Him.* The Bible—often referred to as *His Word*—is clear that "all of us have sinned and fall short of the glory of God" (Romans 3:23). Because of this separation we have what some have called a "God-shaped hole in our hearts" that tells us something is missing—*that something's just not quite right.* Naturally then, we try to find something that will fill that hole.

While coping mechanisms such as alcohol, drugs, food, gambling, shopping, work, money and sex are more obvious in their powerlessness to repair what is truly broken, even many things that are marketed to us as "spiritual" just won't work. Moreover, the "good works" we do in the hope that they will be enough to reconnect us with God when all is said and done at the end of our earthly lives are also incapable of filling that void and bridging the gap. *That is because God is perfect,* (would you want a god who was anything less?), and His standard to bridge the separation caused by sin is *perfection* that none of us can achieve. And while this all may seem hopeless, quite the opposite is true because "while we were still sinners God demonstrated His tremendous love for us" by sending His Son, Jesus—God in human form—to bear the consequences of *all* our sins on Calvary's cross (Romans 5:8). *He did this once and for all.* No other "good works" are necessary although those actions naturally flow out of a heart overcome by thanksgiving once it has accepted what is called the *gift of salvation through faith in Christ* also known as *the Gospel* which means *Good News.*

The Bible tells us that Jesus "stands at the door and knocks" (Revelation 3:20). Ultimately, we are faced with the choice as to whether or not we will let Him in. God, in His love, leaves that decision up to us.

If you have not yet opened the door of your heart by trusting by way of faith in what Jesus accomplished for you on Calvary's cross, would you do so right now? Admit you have sinned, ask for forgiveness and let Jesus be the One to come in and fill that God-shaped hole in your heart as only He can. In doing so you can be assured that you will not only spend eternity with Him but will walk this earth knowing that you are a child of God who is deeply loved. The journey this side of heaven may be filled with tears, but with Christ comes the promise of never walking your road alone. –CHCD

With thanks

In this pursuit to embrace the freedom afforded to us through the God-given gift of tears, I am thankful to many who have lingered with me throughout the various seasons of life.

I believe my precious Judy "Mammy" Snyder spent many hours in prayer asking God to help me take hold of the softer side—suppressed that it was—she knew I had. Thank you, Judy, for never being ashamed to allow your own floodgates to open wide so that others might be touched and cleansed.

The beautiful nurse/missionary, Helen Ellenberger, taught me so much concerning ministry including the undeniable importance of addressing the whole person; indeed, the emotional and the physical are best dealt with when we remember that God created us as spiritual beings.

Linda Tilli's quest to walk in truth and her sold-out desire to seek and know the Person of Jesus Christ is a much needed and ongoing source of confirmation and comfort in my life. Thank you, Linda, for wanting always to go deeper with the Lord and never settling for less than what God wants to give His women.

I am thankful to God for allowing me the privilege of motherhood, the blessing of my precious daughter Molly and the appreciation for real tears that has grown out of our relationship.

Kathleen Brunet Eagan is my editor, but most importantly a friend who has been there for me from the earliest days of my walk with the Lord. Thank you, Kathleen, for your "*Yes, you can*" voice of encouragement and for using your amazing God-given talents to help move me along in His plans for me.

Denise Mitchell Woyke is the friend who lingered with me through some very long and difficult days. You are extraordinarily beautiful, Denise, and I pray you forever walk in that truth.

I am truly blessed by all those who prayed for me during the writing of this book including Sandy Carey, Sonia Greene, Yvonne Shafer, Pat Wenzel and Wendy Zedack. A special thank you to Ellen Greendyk whose five words of encouragement at the onset of this project caused me to go tens of thousands of words.

I am grateful to those who shared their personal stories regarding tears and the many medical professionals who gave of their expertise with specific gratitude to Dr. Elkin A. Nunez as well as my faithful brother-in-Christ Dr. Jose Arrunategui.

Also, I extend a distinctive word of appreciation to William "Bill" H. Frey II, Ph.D., for his ongoing support as I wrestled to understand the science behind the tears.

Thank you to Elise and all the wonderful ladies at my local public library some of whom have let me cry with them.

My heartfelt appreciation to Michael Zedack and John Van Duyne for giving of their talent and to John's daughter Caitlin for being the indispensable force behind the scenes.

Bonnie, Maryann, Julia and Mary, your *very real friendships* are treasured gifts from the Lord.

I am blessed by the special relationships I have gained with Jeannie and Valerie and the lessons in trust and faith we have come to know along the way. Together with these women, I am so very thankful for all my *Moriah* sisters-in-Christ from whom I have learned so much concerning God's love for women.

I give thanks to God for my brothers and sister and their families for demonstrating tremendous love during the exceptionally challenging days we recently faced as a family.

Lastly and significantly, I am grateful to God for my husband Ronald whose ongoing prayers and encouragement resulted in the publishing of this book. Truly *we know that in all things God works for the good of those who love Him, who have been called according to His purpose* (Romans 8:28). –CHCD

Dedication:

In celebration of my mom, Joan Ann Cieciuch, whose suffering truly gave rise to perseverance, character, and a hope that did not disappoint which helped shape me a little bit more into the woman the Lord desires me to be. –CHCD

Table of Contents

Understanding This Book:
Why Should We Cry?

As a girl who grew up on the border of Jersey City, New Jersey who had to learn to be "tough like a boy" (or so I thought), I have spent most of my adult Christian walk desperate to understand true femininity in Christ. Contrary to what I was taught as an undergraduate in my secular women's biblical literature class and, I am sorry to say, by way of some well-intended "religious" teachings, I began to discover that being *female* in Christ meant *freedom to be a woman*. While this statement in its broadest sense is a topic for yet another day, *part of walking in this freedom to be a woman means taking hold of God's gift of tears.* When this truth is embraced, emotions—particularly those connected to suffering—are processed according to God's plan and real unshakable hope comes to life.

This concept was one that took years for me to understand. Indeed, it was not until I experienced the loss of my beautiful friend Donna that I truly began to see what God intends when He extends a special invitation to us to *process* the emotions attached to our tears throughout the various seasons of life, permitting them to run their course so we may ultimately experience the true hope He planned for us in return.

Undeniably, we are created to cry. Even if at this point in your spiritual journey you remain skeptical about God being who Christians profess Him to be, there is no denying that our biological make-up is one that includes *the physiology of crying*. Both men and women are affected. *Yes, real women cry and real men let them because real men cry too*. Some may try to deny this reality and fight back the tears, but still our human bodies naturally continue to call out to us in varying degrees to let them come forth.

That being said, there seems to be great merit in unearthing a deeper understanding of the God ordained role tears were meant to play so we can discover the hope awaiting us through even the most extraordinarily painful circumstances of our lives. In taking on this challenge, I hope to curb some of our well-intended efforts to help the crying person with methods that usually prove detrimental in the long run simply because they have more to do with our personal need *to fix things* than they do with truly addressing the root of one's tears. It is here that men and women often find some of the greatest challenges in their interpersonal relationships.

While this book seeks to embrace the freedom available to us through tears, it is not in any way intended to provide a license for manipulation. *True freedom always involves the truth.* To conjure-up tears in a ploy to get our own way runs contrary to the very avenue of freedom God intended tears to bring. Unfortunately, as I have come to understand more deeply through the research connected to this book, the act of crying in the name of religion and other behaviors connected to "emotional experiences in the name of God," have been sadly exploited. For any who may be familiar with the phrase "the gift of tears" as it relates to ancient monks who encouraged crying as an indication of the depth of one's prayers[1], please know that the purpose of this book is very different for it speaks to how a loving God has designed our bodies to process effectively the seasons in our lives marked by pain and change. *The emphasis here is on the Creator rather than the created.* The presence of God ordained tears is not meant to serve as a spiritual marker of sorts indicating how "holy" or "contrite" we are but as a testimony to the goodness of God. Embracing our God-given gift of tears is not a self-absorbed activity, yet one of *surrender* to the ways of the One Who truly knows what is best.

Finally, if you are among those who have spent much time, attention and study trying to *take charge of your feelings*, please know that this book does not seek to counteract your efforts. Do know, however, that *taking our thoughts captive*[2] doesn't mean shutting down the truth. On the contrary, it means realizing the lies we believe, giving them no authority over our minds and allowing the truth to settle in. In the case of victims who are in process of shaking their minds of the lie that they did something to deserve what happened to them, coming to terms with the truth that they were, in fact, unjustly violated may and most likely will involve tears. Indeed, the emotions that cause our rivers to flow may seem unbearable at times, but the gift awaiting us on the other side is well worth the cost.

CHAPTER ONE:

Permission to Cry

There needs to be a grieving process and the Lord is the One Who carries you through it. And it takes time; it takes time for healing. I've heard many people say who've lost a loved one that in some ways it's like learning to live with an amputation: you do heal, but you're never the same. But I would also say that those who go through this, and trust in the Lord, discover an intimacy with God most people never experience. [3]

Dialogue from the film *Courageous*

It was October, and I had just returned home from our annual women's retreat in the foliage-rich Catskill Mountains. Having spent most of the weekend dealing with the recent death of a friend, I was shocked to find myself seemingly out of nowhere in an emotional pile of tears on my bedroom floor. "What is this?" I asked, almost panic-stricken. "Didn't I just work through my grief?" "Why this?" "Why now?"

I had barely formulated these questions in my mind when I sensed the quiet, compelling, counseling voice of the Holy Spirit—a voice that becomes more and more familiar to us as we spend time getting to know God. Ever so gently He instructed me, "Don't rush this one, Catherine; If you linger with Me in this I will teach you something about Me that you have not known."

While I realized that this was an invitation from God that should not be passed by, I struggled to take hold of my right to accept what He was actually asking: *Linger in grief? Continue to cry?* Such is not the American way in this hurry-up world in which we live, even and, unfortunately at times, in our own church circles. "It's time to march on," we seem to suggest. "We've prayed through all of this, and we need to leave it at the cross. God's will for us is to *overcome* and *walk in victory.* Hasn't He given us dominion over our emotions? Isn't His plan for us to *prosper* and take hold of a life that promises the 'exceedingly, abundantly more than we could ever ask for or imagine?'" [4] For me, all these words required much more energy than I had at the time.

Yes, even in the church, we at times have little patience for grief, or, for that matter, tears. We seem to welcome emotion as a sign of "great movement" on the part of God and as a measuring rod for just how great our worship services are (even though some of these emotions actually have little or nothing to do with worshipping God). But when it truly comes to making a place for *real tears*, few of us are quick to grant permission, especially if the person who is called to linger is oneself. We become apologetic, embarrassed and ashamed by our own emotions. If we happen to be one of the folks sitting next to the hurting person, we become uncomfortable in the awkwardness of the moment and—resorting to what we perceive as *good Christian training*—look to "fix" the situation with some sort of "prescriptural" ointment absent of a true diagnosis. To the hurting person, even our best intentions can amount to little more than "take Psalm 46:10 and call me in the morning." The result is the equivalent of shutting the person down, and all too often to the mind of the one who is hurting, to shut-down is to put-down. Well-intended though they might be, such blanket statements risk making hurting people feel weak in their faith. Likewise, in our own efforts to help one another hurry up and move-on, we risk invalidating the pain and missing the point.

Truly, tears can make us uncomfortable. Even in the women's ministry I oversee I am aware of ladies who have avoided our gatherings because crying and emotions "may happen." Better to leave that cork in the bottle. But now here I was facing this very challenge. A woman. A leader in my church. An overseer's wife who I believe was expected to keep it together. For you see, the friend I lost was loved by more than just me in my church circle. She too was a leader and the wife of an overseer. Our loss was great and women everywhere were looking for help. Our loss was sudden, completely without warning. Tragic, to say the least. A suicide so unexpected that it literally rocked our world.

But I had experienced loss before. In my mind, I was a pro. Beginning with the death of my good friend Lisa when we were both just 11, I had spent much of my life dealing with the tears that accompany this particular kind of pain. Joe died at 19 after a car wreck. Yolande at the age of 23 from cancer. There were of course, my grandparents, my father, Bernie, and my father-like friend, Bill. There were the friends who miscarried or gave birth to still-born children.

So according to my thinking, I should have been an expert at this. But I now realized there was no such thing. Try as we might to prove ourselves otherwise, pastors, pastors' wives, leaders and those we label "professionals" are all people built with bodies designed for tears. We are at times—just like everyone else—called to cry, and to experience its full purpose means giving up our right to decide when this process should be over no matter how many books we've read, (or written), how many degrees we hold or how well we know our Bibles. Our failure to do so ultimately means more trouble down the road. We are at these moments challenged to silence our stock answer of "I know" because we see firsthand that though people may share or identify with someone else's pain, *pain is a remarkably personal experience.*

I could dimly see this because I clearly was not o.k. Still, I challenged my right to feel this way. *What entitled me to embrace an extended period of grief?* Surely, there were others—family—who were closer for whom such a privilege should be reserved. *Truly, I thought, there must be something seriously wrong with my faith if I couldn't pull it together, put this behind me and move on.* Yet, God and my body were telling me otherwise, and giving myself permission to go through this process (for God already had) would be my first true step in understanding the freedom my tears would bring.

In my particular case, it was the loss of this friend that served as the catalyst for granting myself permission to cry. Perhaps in your situation or in the situation of someone you care about it, the experience is similar to mine. On the other hand, maybe the tendency toward tears you are experiencing these days has nothing to do with grief, or so you may think.

On the public-access talk show I co-hosted for fifteen years, I had two opportunities to interview individuals well-versed on the subject of grief: Chris Ann Waters, a bereavement specialist, certified hospice volunteer and author of *Seasons of Goodbye: Working Your Way Through Loss* [5] and Ann Marie Klein, a nurse practitioner with extensive experience in death and dying who serves as a facilitator of a group called *GriefShare.* [6] Both women agree that in the case of the loss of a loved one, grief is a process that should not be short-circuited and allowing someone to go through it is key.

Beyond this, however, Waters notably recognizes that *loss*, and the need to process it, very often applies to situations *which have nothing to do with the death of a loved one.* She is quick to realize *that any kind of loss or change of events*—sudden or otherwise, and, at times, even *planned*—can spur on the type of emotional behaviors typically connected to grief. A divorce, a failed custody battle, a move, the loss of vision or any type of physical challenge that limits us and alters life as we knew it carry with them a moment of awareness whereby we realize that *a loss has occurred and that it should and must be processed.* In most cases, there no doubt will be some level of emotional suffering that in order to be overcome must first be given proper acknowledgment. Waters notes that even situations we commonly perceive as *happy*, like retirement, marriage or graduation, require adjustments—a release of the old (and probably a few tears)—in order to enjoy and embrace the new. In *Seasons of Goodbye*, Waters writes:

> *Endings are as much a part of life as beginnings, but the endings are often harder. They place us in unfamiliar territory emotionally, psychologically, and/or physically. We find ourselves in the unknown as a result of the departure of someone or something known, sometimes deeply known. Paradoxically, that which made us feel joyful and secure can also make us feel sorrowful and insecure when gone. Such insecurity and unfamiliarity because of loss*

brings pain which can only be healed in its own time by the one who bears it, a pain borne by each person in a different way.[7]

As with Waters, Klein not only recognizes the variety of situations that call for some level of grieving but is also much in-tune with the role of tears and the needed release they were meant to provide in processing our losses. As a professional and as a person who has experienced more than one personal tragedy, Klein is quick to confirm that tears are a gift from God that help the hurting person move along in the process of suffering. From pain to healing. From death to life:

Tears in my life have been a poignant part of the healing process from disappointment, personal losses and the starting point for accepting my limitations and being open to the direction God wants to take me. (Specifically), the initial five years following the birth of my first daughter, Sarah, and the subsequent neurological diagnosis of her permanent cognitive and physical impairment sent me into a depression unlike anything I would have ever expected. Tears came often and freely, almost every time I spoke about Sarah in terms of her future. The searing pain of loss brought about by the realization of my daughter going from normal development to the gradual decline of physical/cognitive disabilities made me feel as if the child I had known died and someone replaced her with a total stranger. There was a sense of unfairness and disappoint-ment stemmed from the mommy-induced goals I knew she would not experience: the mother/daughter sharing of secrets and having those special talks, the development of an independent spirit, going to college, developing a career path, and eventually getting married and having children of her own. This reality was replaced by concerns for her safety, her physical care— needs as my husband and I and she grew older. All these issues swirled around in my head often producing a continual burden and frustration with-out answers.

Through my multiple experiences with grief groups, one thing is always the same: tears are the one healing mechanism used to express a variety of feelings associ-ated with the loss and help in the processing of complex emotions.

In The Book of Ecclesiastes, Chapter Three—made famous as a song in the 1960s by the musical group *The Byrds*—the Bible plainly realizes that this side of heaven, there is *a time for everything and a season for every activity: a time to laugh and a time to cry.* [8] In short, crying truly is God ordained. As laughter is the heartfelt response to times of fun and joy, the simple act of crying was intended to provide us with the much needed release for our physically, emotionally and spiritually connected bodies. Therefore, no matter what situation you have faced or are presently facing, the sheer fact that you are *human* [9] has at some point in your journey lent itself to the undeniable truth that your body has prompted you—called out to you—perhaps even *begged you*—to let it cry. It is an important part of how God in His wisdom wired us for survival in this imperfect world in which we live. And, done in the light of God's love for us—no matter how dim that light may sometimes seem—the tears of pain we shed serve as the watering can for the precious seeds sown in seasons of suffering which in time—like any other lovingly and well sown seeds—will ultimately bring forth something real and worth the time and patience it took to bring into being. Maybe all you needed was for someone to tell you it was o.k. to start sowing, someone to give you permission to cry. God's design of our bodies says He already has.

CHAPTER TWO:

Some of the Real Science
Behind the Tears of Real Women

The many critical functions of tears in the body are discussed from an intelligent design worldview. As more research is carried out, often what once were felt to be "simple structures" in biology turn out to be extremely complex. Research has now shown that tears are a complex fluid that is required for long-term vision. Furthermore, although all animals that live in the atmosphere and possess eyes produce tears, only humans can shed emotional tears—a response that has been found to have several health benefits. This fact is indicative of one more difference between humans and animals. [10]

Dr. Jerry Bergman, *Biologist*

Since the aim of this book is to help women embrace the God-given gift of tears and their role in processing our emotions, a brief overview of the amazing design of our bodies and how and why tears are generated seems in order.

In short science identifies three individual types of tears: *basal*, which are the tears that lubricate the eyes; *reflex*, which are generated in response to an irritant such as pollen or a poke in the eye; and *physic* or *emotional* tears which may be triggered by conditions such as stress, suffering, physical pain and—as we saw in our discussion of *loss* in Chapter One—even situations commonly perceived as happy. [11]

Of specific and fascinating interest regarding the classification of tears is the realization by physiologists and ophthalmologists alike that not only do we produce tears for different reasons, *but the very chemical composition of tears are varied and unique to the situation for which they are produced.* [12] (More on this topic in the chapter which follows.)

Regardless of their classification and function, all of these tears are produced by way of the *lacrimal system* which is made up of *glands*. The tears are then drained out of the eyes through tiny openings called the *puncta*, which are found along the eyelids close to the nose. They then move into the small canals in the lids into the lacrimal sac which is beneath the skin on each side of the nose. From there tears are transported down the tear duct and emptied into the back of the nose and throat. This is the reason why you may get a runny nose when you cry. [13]

The physical benefits to such a design are significant. The lubricant effect of basal tears keeps the eyes from becoming dry and uncomfortable. The production of reflex tears helps guard against infection. [14] In His book, *Crying: The Natural and Cultural History of Tears*, author Tom Lutz recognizes, "The cornea of the eye has a far from perfect surface. It is pocked, wrinkled, uneven. Tears smooth out these irregularities in the surface of the eye and thus make possible vision as we know it. Without this everyday teary layer, we would see a world of weird diffractions and absences, (and) be unable to move our eyes." [15]

For most people, this system of bringing forth tears is the norm and therefore often taken for granted. There are, however, times when either an abundance of tears or a complete absence of them creates challenging situations. I, for one, have learned by personal experience that normal tear production, which sometimes seems like more of an annoyance that needs to be stopped at any cost, is in fact the true miracle of God that science reveals it to be.

In 2001 my daughter Molly was born with *overflow tearing* caused by what is commonly referred to as *blocked* (or *clogged*) *tear ducts*. The American Academy of Ophthalmology (AAO) recognizes that this condition occurs when a membrane (piece of tissue) at the end of the tear duct that should open before birth stays closed prohibiting tears from draining properly though the duct into the back of the nose and throat. [16]

While the blockage may open on its own as the infant begins to grow, some cases require opening the ducts by passing a probe through the tear drain. If that is not successful, additional surgery may be required. [17]

Because of this condition—particularly in the earliest years of her life—Molly was prone to both eye mucous discharge and infection. On more mornings than I would like to remember, she awoke barely able to see with her eyelashes tightly stuck together by a yellow secretion rivaling the adhesive power of superglue. Indeed such a sight is heartbreaking to a new mother, causing me in turn to expel a few real tears of my own.

While clogged tear ducts are not uncommon among newborns, it should be noted that the challenges connected to them are not limited to the very young as some individuals develop similar problems later in life. My friend Cheri's very serious issues with her tear ducts began when all three of her children were already into their teenaged years:

> *I teach grammar to middle school students and in the early Spring of 2011 I noticed that my right eye was tearing a lot although at the time I was completely unaware that it was an abnormal situation.*
>
> *At first it was once in a while, but after a few weeks it became a constant flow and got to the point where the vision in my right eye was often cloudy. I literally carried*

a tissue in my hand at all times and the skin around my eye was red and raw from the constant wiping and drying of the tears.

After about 3 months, it had gotten to the point where my eye was crusty every morning when I woke up, and it seemed as though the eye was actually lower on my face, which I learned later it was! At this point I decided to make an appointment with the ophthalmologist because the issue had become so bothersome, and my eyesight was really being affected.

The ophthalmologist suggested antibiotic eye drops for a clogged tear duct, but felt it would not clear the clog. After three weeks I returned, and he attempted to use a syringe full of some special fluid to "flush" the duct. This was rather unsuccessful! The doctor suggested I see a specialist in eye surgery who almost immediately suggested an issue with the sinus as the cause of the blocked tear duct. He then sent me to an ENT who sent me for an MRI of the sinuses: the results were not good! I had a cyst on the sinus bone which was pressing on the canal of the tear duct causing a block, and this would have to be surgically removed. The surgery took place in October of 2011, so at this point I had been dealing with this discomfort for 6 months.

The surgery was successful, I guess. The tear duct, although not "blocked" any more, still occasionally tears due to pressure from the sinuses which have continued to be a problem. A strict change in diet and most likely one more sinus surgery will clear this up.

I truly never realized how much I took my natural tearing process for granted. When it flowed constantly I knew something was seriously wrong, and it was very frustrating, until I found out what the problem was and had it fixed. Every time my eye tears now I know it is a sign that I have heavy sinus congestion or an infection starting. Kind of neat how our body can tell us something when we pay attention to it!

While Cheri's experience with overflow tearing presented its own set of challenges, still others suffer as a result of conditions that are directly the opposite from hers. *Dry Eye Syndrome* occurs when the lacrimal glands do not bring forth sufficient tears to moisturize the surface of the eye. Sufferers of this condition can find it tremendously painful. While there are a variety of reasons individuals develop *Dry Eye*, it is worth mentioning that this condition is more common in women—postmenopausal women, to be exact. [18]

Along the same lines as Dry Eye is a condition known as *alacrima*. Common in individuals with certain disorders or isolated congenital defects, *alacrima* is defined as "a deficiency or absence of the secretion of tears."[19] Yet again, such a topic hits very close to home.

While our daughter's pediatric ophthalmologist has told us that Molly's ducts are no longer clogged and that she produces sufficient amounts of lubricating tears to maintain the health of her eyes, Molly—for unknown reasons—shows signs of alacrima in that *she does not bring forth emotional tears when she is crying.*[20] Because of this—with a few odd exceptions in her infancy that involved one or two drops—I have never had the experience of watching my daughter emotionally relieve herself by way of an actual stream of tears and the beauty of their cleansing qualities. Instead, Molly's tears appear to be trapped beneath the surface. During emotional moments when she is clearly crying, her face develops a red-spotted measles-like appearance in the absence of emotional tears.

With such an observation a notable distinction is formed: while tears were intended to be excreted during crying, it is possible to cry without the actual "shedding" of tears. In Molly's case, her inability to release emotional tears when needed causes her face to take on the look of pressure being built up, which interestingly is exactly the way some people— who want or need to cry but for some reason can or will not— often feel on the inside. In short—to this mom, anyway—the marvelous interconnection of God's design between the physical and emotional release becomes undeniable. Clearly, tears were intended to do their job, inside and out.

CHAPTER THREE:

Emotional Tears
and the Female Body

*We were not surprised when we compiled data from
the approximately 1500 crying episodes in the crying dia-
ries and found that women cry more than men. Our study
conclusively confirmed the widely-held belief that females
do indeed shed more tears, more often than males.* [21]

William H. Frey II, Ph.D.
Crying: The Mystery of Tears

Most of us would agree—with or without scientifically gath-
ered evidence in hand—that *women simply cry more than men.*
Indeed, the cosmetic industry has capitalized on this fact as
makeup aisles and cosmetic counters host brand after brand
of waterproof mascara. Likewise, tissue manufactures are on
top of this information clearly targeting the female consumer
by way of some of their packaging (just check out the designs
online at the *Kleenex Style Studio*). In this age of theatre-sized

television screens hung-high in the modern "man cave," many women are more apt to opt for dinner out with a friend followed by a showing of the genre of movie commonly known as a "chick-flick." (Not my favorite phrase.) In short, these "flicks" are films that simply are more likely to resonate with women than men. They are movies like *Steel Magnolias* and *Beaches* during which *women cry*. The actresses themselves cry, and with our travel-sized tissues in hand, we cry with them. We cry because we know what it is like to have a sick child. We cry because our own friend may be hurting. *We cry because we are women and when other women cry, we cry, too.* Then again there are those women—knowing they will cry and would rather not—who make deliberate efforts to avoid such films. A decision to go or not to go, to cry or not to cry, may of course be specifically linked to where such a woman happens to be along her own path of pain and change.

Despite our general acceptance of this information, misunderstandings, intolerance and awkwardness between men and women in response to female tears no doubt continues to challenge the sexes. Worth mentioning, this is not due to an absence of scientific attempts like that of Dr. Frey's to develop a truer understanding of the workings of emotional tears in the human body.

For centuries, many believed that tears came directly from the brain and were connected to *humors* (body fluids which include blood, phlegm and two forms of bile) that were believed to determine the state of one's overall health. [22] It was within this line of thinking that techniques such as the use of leeches to "purge" oneself of excess fluids came into being.

Hundreds of years later, in the late 1700s, tears and their relationship to the lacrimal system were discovered. [23] In the first half of the twentieth century, early investigations of the hormone-releasing endocrine glands and attention to the modern physiology of emotions would open the door to a variety of fascinating discoveries regarding the interconnection between the brain and emotional experience. [24] And while some of the science regarding emotional tears is still unknown, it is well accepted that these tears and other emotional experiences do involve both the limbic system of the brain otherwise known as the "emotional brain" as well as the endocrine system and its hormones. [25] Though this might not come as a surprise to those who randomly attribute hormones to what may be "wrong" with women and as a blanket explanation as to why we may cry at the drop-of-a-hat, a proper understanding of the subject calls for a better explanation of what hormones actually are, the roles they were designed to carry out in our human bodies and their place in bringing forth emotional tears.

According to *MedlinePlus*, an online publication of the National Institutes of Health (NIH), *hormones are your body's chemical messengers.* The production of these substances are most notably associated with the endocrine glands including the pituitary, pineal, thymus, thyroid, adrenal glands and pancreas. Additionally, men make hormones in their testes and women make them in their ovaries. [26] Beyond this more commonly known information, Dr. Frey's detailed study on crying in the 1980s showed hormones are also produced in the acinar cells located within the lacrimal gland. [27]

Though small in size, hormones are powerful in substance. Traveling into the bloodstream to tissues or organs, hormones work slowly, over time, and impact many different bodily functions including growth and development, metabolism, sexual function, reproduction and, yes, mood. [28]

The NIH recognizes that it takes only a tiny amount of hormones to trigger significant changes in how the body functions. It reports that this is the reason too much or too little of a certain hormone *can be serious.*

I personally learned this lesson when my mother ended up in the emergency room after we were unable to wake her up from what appeared to be a very deep sleep. To my surprise one of the first doctors to appear in the ER on her behalf was an endocrinologist—a doctor specifically trained to treat hormone imbalances. No doubt he was on the scene to investigate my mother's history of hypothyroidism. A common and sometimes misdiagnosed problem in women, hypothyroidism occurs when the thyroid gland does not produce enough of the thyroid hormone known as levothyroxine. Without this hormone, the body cannot function properly. Insufficient levels can result in symptoms that include a reduction in energy levels, depression, weight gain, hair loss, drying skin and greater sensitivity to cold. [29]

Having dealt with hypothyroid issues of my own, (yes, it can be hereditary), I initially was unable to grasp why—in what truly seemed to be an urgent situation—such attention was being paid to a condition that was usually regulated by one tiny pill a day. Tests quickly proved that my mother was in fact in a state known as *myxedema coma*. Occurring when thyroid hormone levels get extremely low, *myxedema coma* is the most severe and rarest form of hypothyroidism and is considered a medical emergency. Patients suffering from this condition may require oxygen, breathing (ventilator) assistance, fluid replacement and intensive-care nursing. [30] Sure enough in this particular case, a trip to the ICU for several days would be the course of treatment for my mom.

While changes in hormone levels are significant enough to create crisis situations like this, these same tiny substances play key roles in our ability to produce tears. Elevated thyroid secretion causes an increase in tears while degeneration of the gland can greatly inhibit tear production. [31] Also, the hormone *prolactin*—produced in both the pituitary and lacrimal glands—has specifically been shown to play a critical part in the body's ability to make tears. In fact, findings by Dr. Frey show this hormone is actually present in the chemical composition of emotional tears. [32] And while this is true for both men and women, this particular hormone holds special significance regarding a variety of functions associated with the female body.

Increasing in girls around puberty (while decreasing in boys), prolactin helps develop breast tissue and works within the ovaries following ovulation to produce the hormones progesterone and estrogen. As its name suggests, it is this hormone that is primarily responsible for prompting and supporting supplies of milk production (lactation). Not surprisingly then, serum prolactin levels are significantly higher in women than they are in men and increase dramatically during pregnancy. [33]

Specific to the role of prolactin and the production of tears in the female body, Dr. Frey's study documented increased episodes of crying in women right around the time of ovulation—13-16 days after the onset of menstruation [34]—a time in which my own gynecologist has told me both estrogen and prolactin are elevated. [35] In contrast, postmenopausal women with significantly decreased prolactin and estrogen levels are most likely to suffer from Dry Eye Syndrome. [36]

Although further study is necessary regarding a specific link, Dr. Frey references one individual's experience concerning frequent emotional crying and a condition known as hyperprolactinemia in which prolactin levels are severely elevated. [37] According to the American Society for Reproductive Medicine, hyperprolactinemia is relatively common in women, and about a third of women in their childbearing years with irregular periods but normal ovaries experience this condition.

When this happens, a woman might have trouble getting pregnant. Markedly, hypothyroidism may also cause hyperprolactinemia. [38] In both of these diagnoses, depression can be an issue. Notably, when the hyperprolactinemia was successfully treated in the individual reporting her experience to Dr. Frey, the excessive crying stopped.

Additional findings from current studies attribute clear distinctions between the male and female lacrimal systems as a result of the hormone prolactin. Dr. Frey notes:

> *Since I wrote my book, several key discoveries have been made. It is clear now that the male and female lacrimal glands are anatomically different.* [39] *Further, even before my book was written, an article by Martinazzi and Baroni* [40] *showed that the gender difference between the male and female lacrimal glands of mice was determined in large part by the hormone prolactin derived from the pituitary gland. In other words, we are not surprised that women can nurse infants and men cannot because we can see that the female breast (mammary gland) is structurally different from that of the male breast. Similarly, the female tear glands are anatomically, structurally different from those of males and this difference is due in part to the effects of the hormone prolactin.* [41]

Consistent with these discoveries, Dr. Frey believes it is highly likely that there is a biological (morphologic and hormonal) reason why women cry more than men.

Much remains to be unearthed regarding the presence of prolactin in emotional tears. However, its function in developing distinctly female tear glands reinforces the age-old truth that while equally created by God, men and women are not made the same. How amazing it is to realize that one tiny hormone key to the development of a woman's body also lends itself to the very manner by which we bring forth distinctly female tears. Such a design was no doubt intentional and calls attention to both our unique qualities as women and the extraordinary role tears are meant to fulfill throughout the seasons of our lives.

CHAPTER FOUR:

The Benefit of a
Good Old-Fashioned Meltdown

Tears are an amazing mechanism put in place as a remarkable demonstration of God's care for us in dealing with the day-to-day issues of life. It is a spring valve which allows the outpouring of our expression of emotion. It's our opportunity of cleansing off the spiritual heaviness of burdens. It's our outlet of pent up frustration, anger and lack of control over events and circumstances in our lives. It's our expression of joy as well as grief.

Ann Marie Klein BSN, RN, NP

Before the ink had dried on the very first pages of my introduction for this book, I told a woman in my Bible study that I was writing a book on how I believed God gave women the gift of tears. To my surprise, without missing a beat, her immediate response was to ask me: "And how healing is that?" That became just the affirmation I needed to move forward in this task. Without any data in hand, this woman, a wife and a mother, simply knew that there was a special link between our physical ability to bring forth tears and the benefit of healing it somehow carries.

Indeed emotional tears in and of themselves are truly a therapeutic miracle for as I learned through the research connected to this book, *they are so much more than just a drop of salty water.* As the properties of reflex and irritant tears lubricate, refresh, guard against infection and help bring clarity, some researchers like Dr. Frey theorize that emotional tears also carry with them valuable ingredients associated with the process of detoxification. [42] Moreover, in addition to the hormone prolactin, Dr. Frey's study found that emotional tears contain adrenocorticotropic hormone (ACTH) and leucine encephalin (an endorphin and natural opiate) which are released in the body during times of stress. [43]

While more research is needed regarding the chemicals found in emotional tears and their specific role in relieving stress, in most cases—particularly on days where absolutely *nothing* seems to go right—a good cry simply helps us to feel better. And while those of us who have benefited from a "good old-fashioned meltdown" recognize this fact, Dr. Frey's study was the first to confirm scientifically that people feel better after crying as a whopping 85 percent of women and 73 percent of men who recorded personal episodes of crying reported feeling better afterward. [44] Because people reported feeling less angry and less sad once they had shed some tears, Dr. Frey concluded the widely held belief that "crying does appear to alleviate stress" and called emotional tears "a direct biological and normal human response to emotional stress." [45] Moreover, having done ground-breaking research in a variety of areas concerning the brain in his role as founder and co-director of the Alzheimer's Research Center at Regions Hospital in St. Paul MN, Dr. Frey also notes, "Crying is another way of protecting the brain by alleviating stress." [46]

Beyond this information, a vast array of professionals in a variety of fields have also investigated and documented their own findings concerning the benefits of emotional crying. Writing in the 1960s and 1970s, psychologist Silvan Tomkins developed a theory of crying based on the belief that while a person can decisively give way to tears in the hope of being comforted, crying is sometimes an "involuntarily response" by the nervous system in its efforts to return the body to a place of rest and relief. [47] In 2008, a team of psychologists at the University of South Florida and Tilburg University in the Netherlands lent credence to Tomkins' theory when its evaluation of more than 3,000 occurrences of crying showed that this type of release does play a significant role in returning the body to a more restful state by helping to control breathing. [48] The team also affirmed the findings of Dr. Frey by reporting that the majority of those who participated in its study experienced feeling emotionally better after shedding some tears.

A variety of women nurses have also made contributions to the understanding of the role of emotional tears. In addition to the opening quote for this chapter penned by nurse practitioner and close friend, Ann Marie Klein, an article titled "The Healing Effect of Tears" by Marjaneh M. Fooladi—also a nurse—seeks to put into perspective the multiple benefits associated with crying. Having reviewed the findings of Dr. Frey and others who have investigated crying, Fooladi tells the nursing community that "tears appear to play a significant role in detoxification of the body and enhancement of mental well-being." [49] In an article titled "Crying: The Neglected Dimension" published in 1976 in *The Canadian Nurse*, Abigail McGreevy and Judy Van Heukelem outline how nurses can assist patients suffering from anxiety who are having difficulty crying to meet their need to bring forth emotional tears. [50] In an abstract on this same issue published in the *Journal of Psychology and Theology*, Van Heukelem notes, "The expression of pain, whether physical, emotional, or spiritual, in the form of tears is often difficult for the professional helper to deal with. The role of the counselor is to support and encourage crying rather than to inhibit or 'put it down' as a sign of instability or spiritual immaturity." [51]

And then there are the testimonies of medical professionals who clearly recognize the association between a good-old fashioned meltdown and the various seasons of change in the female body like OB/GYN Dr. Jose Arrunategui—a diplomat of the American Board of Obstetrics and Gynecology—whom I have been blessed to know for more than 20 years. During my own pregnancy, it was Dr. Arrunategui's quick, professional and personal intervention that saved my daughter Molly's life.

Encountering more women than he could probably ever count in his nearly 30 years of practice and having a wife and four daughters of his own (as well as three boys!), Dr. Arrunategui is excessively familiar with the seasons of change that accompany a woman's life as well as the relationship these seasons have to the onset of tears. Notably, he recognizes the varied function of prolactin in tear production, stress and the various stages of development of the female body and personally believes increased amounts of prolactin in emotional tears is an indicator of the elevated serum level of this hormone in times of stress.

Of specific interest, Dr. Arrunategui believes that women become emotionally susceptible to tears during seasons of transition because these are stressing times of change physically, hormonally, emotionally and psychologically. He furthers this point citing specific examples of transition including "a young girl becoming a lady; a beautiful slim young (pregnant) lady morphing into 30-40 extra pounds with top risen estrogen, progesterone and prolactin who is about to sign a contract for nearly two decades to take care of that little person coming; a 40 or 50 something, sexually competent woman getting in a season of hormonal and in many cases sexual decay, with a husband possibly getting into a middle-age crisis and parents that are ill or dying."

Between these lines the subject of *loss* once again rises to the surface as such examples clearly indicate the arrival of seasons of change with which women must come to terms. While puberty looks to the celebration of becoming a woman and the soon-to-be coolness of wearing lip gloss and heels, entering the realms of womanhood brings with it the loss of the little girl. While pregnancy longs to hold the child, it recognizes that life will never be the same and the loss (at least temporarily) of a smaller waist line. For many, perimenopause and menopause signal the passing of youth and physical beauty. As with similar situations spoken of earlier, effectively processing these losses will in many cases involve crying. Emotional tears in response to these seasons of change may be a result of feelings of frustration, anger, shifting hormones and, at times, utter hopelessness over that which we feel we have no control.

Specifically in the case of perimenopausal and menopausal women, all too often hopelessness is fueled by a new or renewed sense of *worthlessness*. With our changing body comes losses in previously known identities as grown children leave the home and duties shift to the role of caregiver to aging parents. Some women in this situation become especially susceptible to depression which left unchecked can become serious.

Having served as an instructor for a continuing education class designed to help students enter or re-enter the technology driven workforce, I found that among my middle-aged students—all of whom were women—there existed a deep struggle for identity. In the little that I have witnessed and have come to know from my menopausal friends, the sense of unworthiness is at times magnified. Many of these women are simply looking for someone safe who *gets it* with whom they can just have a good old-fashioned meltdown and ultimately be reassured of their tremendous worth and value.

An awareness of these truths is critical to us as women if we are to lead emotionally and spiritually healthy lives as we advance from one season to the next. Rather than fight or try to deny that which is inevitable for all of us this side of eternity, coming to terms with the role of tears as it relates to the changes in our female bodies means embracing the healing power of this gift for all it was truly meant to be. Whether by way of a private moment alone or in the safety of one who will allow us to let our tears run their course, a good-old fashioned meltdown may indeed work wonders in shattering the ugly lies that work hard to destroy the beauty that can be ours as we move from one season to the next.

CHAPTER FIVE:

How God Sees and Responds to Our Tears

He heals the brokenhearted and binds up their wounds. He determines the number of the stars and calls them each by name."

Psalm 147:3-4

Psalm 147:4 is one of my favorite Bible verses. At first glance, this line of Scripture may seem to have little or no relationship to the sentence proceeding it. However, as with all things orchestrated by a loving and purposeful God, such is not the case.

Following a verse which speaks about God "healing the brokenhearted and binding up their wounds," the psalmist goes on to tell us that God "determines the number of stars and calls them each by name." The placing of these phrases is noteworthy as it is intended to bring together the characteristics of

God as One Who is compassionate, responds to suffering and has a keen eye for detail.

In creating the universe, God took deliberate action to ensure that each and every star had its own name by which it would be called forth to light up the sky. In naming them, God personalized the stars, thus calling attention to their value. Significantly, this is the very same God Who is in the business of healing our emotional wounds. As with the stars, God knows and calls us each by name. [52] And, He counts every tear.

As the writer of Psalm 56, King David clearly knew this. In a moment of dire need (captivity) and believing in what this Scripture calls "a record of tears," David asks God to "list" his tears upon His "scroll." In some translations, this "scroll" is also called a "wineskin" or "bottle." Elaborating on this in her book, *A Place of Healing: Wrestling with the Mysteries of Suffering, Pain, and God's Sovereignty*, author Joni Eareckson Tada, a quadriplegic intimately familiar with suffering and the depth that processing its associated change can bring, tells us:

> *Remember, (God) places your tears in His bottle. Now there's a reason God's Word describes it that way— because in a bottle, our tears won't evaporate.* [53]

Yes, God collects our tears, and as Tada and King David realize, He does so in such a manner that they will not be forgotten thus magnifying their value. Like the stars, each one is accounted for. As they trickle or pour forth down our cheeks, each drop is met by a loving God who understands the undeniable need for humankind to express itself emotionally through tears. As a God of great patience, at no time during His collection does He look to push us prematurely through the process. On the contrary, in speaking to those who have long been waiting for God to respond to their cries for help, the prophet Isaiah explains that while the season of suffering they are enduring appears unnoticed by God, quite the opposite is true. And, like the psalmist, Isaiah once again calls attention to the stars to signify that what appears to be apathy on God's part is really an opportunity to demonstrate His tremendous patience toward our ongoing cries in times of extended pain:

> *Lift your eyes and look to the heavens: Who created all these? He Who brings out the starry host one by one, and calls them each by name. Because of His great power and mighty strength, not one of them is missing. Why do you say, O Jacob, and complain, O Israel, "My way is hidden from the Lord; my cause is disregarded by my God"? Do you not know? Have you not heard? The Lord is the everlasting God, the Creator of the ends of the earth. He will not grow tired or weary, and His understanding no one can fathom.* [54]

Consequently, though some seasons of suffering may feel long and slow-moving, solace may be found in God's ongoing desire to be with us in these moments no matter how long our present situation may last. Though we as people may give way to frustration in our inability to change the circumstances of our present condition, God quietly hovers over us catching our tears as they fall. Not only does He see and account for these tears, but He also hears the prayers that accompany them whether they come in the form of ear piercing shouts or inaudible groans that only He as Creator can understand. Again and again throughout Scripture, we see evidence of this truth.

In 2 Kings 20:5 word is sent to a "bitterly weeping" Hezekiah, ruler of Judah, who "became ill and was at the point of death," to let him know that God has heard his prayers and seen his tears;

In a story known for intense suffering as the result of tremendous loss, a heartbroken man named Job declares that God is both His "intercessor and his friend" as he "pours out tears" to Him. [55]

Psalm 116, a beautiful portrayal of a loving God who "hears" and "turns His ear toward the cry of those who call out for mercy," speaks specifically to delivering the writer's "eyes from tears." And, as its name suggests, the Old Testament Book of Lamentations, written by Jeremiah known as "the weeping prophet," is devoted almost entirely to the subject of tears.

Beyond these stories and verses born out of situations connected to men and at a time when women were often culturally perceived and treated as inferior, God shattered stereotypes and the lies that accompanied them by ascribing unquestionable value to the tears of women. There is the recognition of the "tears of Rachel crying for her children" spoken about by the prophet Isaiah. There is notice of Hannah's tears—which we will speak of again in Chapter Nine—to which God responds by granting her a son. In Luke 7 a "sinful" woman seemingly unworthy of attention by the elite dinner crowd instead was recognized by Jesus as one who "loved much" for washing His feet with her tears. And, in what I perceive as one of the greatest living Biblical pictures of God's thoughts toward women, the first appearance and recorded words of the risen Christ occur in direct response to the tears of a grieving woman when He asks Mary Magdalene, *"Woman, why are you crying?"* Indeed, the God of the universe shows great interest in our tears and is likewise ready to meet us in the midst of them. Sometimes, as with Mary, such a meeting comes in completely unexpected and extraordinary ways.

Without a doubt, our emotional tears do not come as a surprise to the Creator God. In our moments of need, He is right there with us, and it is often in these very times of tears that a door opens for us to know Him so intimately that the reality of His quiet presence is unmistakable. Though we may not always be able to put it into words, *we somehow just know,* as Psalm 46 reveals, *that God is an ever-present help in trouble.* In the times when others might misunderstand the cries of our heart and the tears that accompany them, God in His love longs to come alongside of us in our pain as no one else can.

As we respond to His quiet nudges to draw near to Him, our suffering can begin to make sense in the security of the One Scripture calls "the friend Who sticks closer than a brother." [56] In the moments that I have allowed God in during my own seasons of pain, He has made it clear to me—usually a step at a time—when it is time to move forward into a place of healing. He has never condemned or despised the tears brought to Him in seasons of pain and change even when I condemned myself for my inability to just get over it and move on as the current worldly mindset would have me do. Oftentimes I find that it is God Who is patiently waiting for me to permit myself to cry so that He might get to the true purpose of this season. While the circumstance which created it may indeed be tragic, God in His promise to waste nothing [57] can use it to heal deeper wounds that may have been there for generations.

But what about those seasons of pain that never seem to end? And how about that age-old question as to why a loving God would allow such suffering in the first place?

In the course of writing this chapter, I became keenly aware that prior to what is known as "the fall of man" in Genesis 3, *there was no need for emotional tears in response to suffering for sin had not yet entered the world.* Taking into account man's disobedience toward God, *the first of those tears no doubt came as a result of all the losses which followed.* Adam and Eve suffered the loss of a magnificently perfect garden, a life free from the grind of work, and living forever never having to face illness. Most significantly of all, they lost the special intimacy with the Creator Himself as sin caused man to be separated from God. As a result, emotional tears of pain and suffering began to fall.

While this news may cause dismay, it is important to realize that this account in Genesis *immediately* follows with a message of God's undeserved grace and favor. Even though it was humankind, *not God*, who messed up and brought suffering into the world, man was instantly met by a loving God Who brought forth an on-the-spot promise of redemption and restoration. Speaking to the serpent, which in this story represents Satan and the mastermind behind the plot to separate God from man, God declares, "I will put enmity (meaning "hatred" in Hebrew) between you and the woman, and between your offspring and hers; he will crush your head, and you will strike his heel." [58]

Yes, as emotional tears began to flow, God in His love brought forth the promise of One Who would be born of a woman—a Savior—Who would reverse the curse and rightfully restore the relationship between God and man. Commentary on the website *Answers in Genesis* furthers this point:

> *That the Seed would bruise the serpent's head is the most important part of the promise. This bruising was more than just a simple pool of blood trapped underneath the skin. 1 John 3:8 states that Christ came into the world*

to destroy the devil's work. The bruising of the serpent's head is symbolic of Christ's victory over Satan. [59]

Though His incarnation would not occur until centuries after the fall of man, people of the Old Testament rode the coattails of these assurances, and by faith "received what was promised" [60] by believing in the One Who was to come. Unlike some of the "faith" messages that promote a strategy of "believe as hard as you can, and you'll get whatever you want," which reduces the character of God to some kind of genie at our disposal to grant our every wish (just think what would happen if we said "yes" to everything our kids asked us for!), the cries depicted throughout the Old Testament are an exercise in *real faith*. They demonstrate an un-muddied belief in the existence of a God and the promise of a Savior they could not see. Such is a necessary condition for receiving the reward of comfort that only God can bring: *And without faith it is impossible to please God, because anyone who comes to him must believe that he exists and that he rewards those who earnestly seek him.* (Hebrews 11:6)

With such a faith, the people "cried out" to God in their pain. And though not all of the individual references to "crying" in the Old Testament tell us if the situation included the presence of emotional tears without investigation into the original language (there are numerous Hebrew words used in the Old Testament to describe *crying*), all are important in their demonstration of the undeniable presence of a merciful God in times of emotional distress:

> *The Lord said, "I have indeed seen the misery of my people in Egypt. I have heard them crying out because of their slave drivers, and I am concerned about their suffering."* Exodus 3:7

> *...when we cried out to the Lord, he heard our cry and sent an angel and brought us out of Egypt.* Numbers 20:16

> *In my distress I called to the Lord; I called out to my God. From his temple he heard my voice; my cry came to his ears.* 2 Samuel 22:7, Psalm 18:6

> *You saw the suffering of our ancestors in Egypt; you heard their cry at the Red Sea. For he has not despised or scorned the suffering of the afflicted one; he has not hidden his face from him but has listened to his cry for help.* Nehemiah 9:9

> *The eyes of the Lord are on the righteous, and his ears are attentive to their cry.* Psalm 34:15

In our seasons of pain, we can by faith—as with the people of long ago—know a loving God who sees and responds to our tears. We can rest assured, as He would have us do, that in those times when we feel that our cries do nothing more than hit the air and return unanswered that they are instead coming before the ears of One Who is listening more closely to our heart than any other person, no matter how gifted or compassionate that person may be. Ultimately, in keeping with His promises, the same God Who "determines the number of stars and calls them out by name" will take that which we bring to Him through tears and "bind up our broken hearts and heal all our wounds." In His perfect time, the God Who sees and responds to our tears will work even the most painful circumstances to our good according to His purpose. [61] Through Jesus, the Savior born of a woman sent to crush the head of the serpent and redeem us from the separation caused by the fall, we are promised the "good news" delivered by the prophet, Isaiah, centuries long ago:

> *He has sent me to bind up the brokenhearted...to comfort all who mourn, and provide for those who grieve in Zion—to bestow on them a crown of beauty instead of ashes, the oil of gladness instead of mourning, and a garment of praise instead of a spirit of despair.* [62]

CHAPTER SIX:

We Were Designed to Cry: So Why Do We Fight Back the Tears?

I rarely cried before Christ. I had to be strong all the time because no one cared for or protected the little girl within. I wanted the qualities men possessed and had no desire to behave like a woman. Softness/gentleness were ingredients for mistreatment, and how much more abuse could I endure? But when Christ penetrated my wounded heart with His great love, tears began to pour from my eyes.

Jennifer Davidson

While God the Creator and scientists alike recognize the unique role of crying in processing pain and relieving suffering, there remain women like Jennifer who have refused to make room for emotional tears. As a teenager who endured various kinds of abuse, fighting back her tears was to Jennifer one important weapon in an arsenal amassed for her survival. Fearing that she might be misunderstood, or worse, an easy target for yet more abuse by those who might capitalize on what she perceived as weakness, Jennifer held high her armor in her all-out war against tears. Simply put, she remained in battle mode because she just didn't feel safe.

While survival techniques such as Jennifer's are all too common, it is important to note that not everyone who makes determined efforts to shut down the tears comes from a background of blatant abuse. Buying into what others have pitched to us as appropriate responses from their personal rule book regarding the governance of tears (which they, of course, acquired from someone else), the unnatural act of suppressing tears is at its root a learned behavior for people from all walks of life. Sadly then, responses like Jennifer's are falsely based on a fear of what others will think (people-pleasing) and fueled by a distorted definition of what "healthy" is supposed to look like. As Dr. Frey has said, "People have the right to be human, to feel, to cry. They need to know there is no need to deprive themselves of the natural healthy release of emotional tears... (However) because of parental, peer and societal pressure, many humans have taught themselves to suppress their emotional tears." [63]

While we may not immediately recognize it, imposing conditions on someone else's God-given right to process emotional suffering with the help of tears is a form of manipulation. It is within this line of thinking that the victim state is reinforced as the opinions of others are given ongoing power over our lives. It is also within this realm that we begin to seek out alternate ways of silencing our pain. In doing so we risk opening the door for addictions to take root as we begin to substitute the love of God with other kinds of "relief."

For too many women of all ages, food (or the lack thereof) is looked upon as an easy, immediate and legal source of comfort. Though initially seen as a harmless way to help us through our pain, addictions connected to food may result in tremendous physical and psychological problems down the road causing some women to end up utterly despising themselves.

In addition to this issue, and, despite wide-spread education and good intentions through a vast array of programs, substance addictions to alcohol and drugs remain serious issues in the twenty-first century. As our pain begins to cry out louder and louder for attention, what started out as just having a drink or two to "take the edge off" can suddenly morph into the consumption of an entire bottle of alcohol. Shockingly in today's world, the use of heroin—a powerful drug that does not discriminate between poor teenagers and rich celebrities—is on the rise. [64] And, in a world where the Internet has become increasingly available "on-demand," vulnerability to process addictions such as pornography and gambling loom large. In this age of "social networking," opportunities abound for a variety of tech-driven sexual addictions that have the capacity to destroy families. Somehow, often without any real sense of how it happened, attempts to escape and silence our pain quietly gain control over our lives. Indeed, the quest to keep the tears at bay and the poor choices this requires does little more than compound the problem.

While it may not be immediately obvious to some who would not call themselves chronic overeaters, anorexic/bulimic, alcoholics, gamblers or Internet sex addicts, efforts to bypass pain are prolific in today's high-tech, fast-moving, give-it-to-me-now, "just get on with it" world in which we live where we simply do not have time for tears. Moreover, in this present age of entitlement, we somehow have falsely come to believe that we have the right to be excused from our personal responsibility to properly address pain. Our diluted notions of "hurry up and survive" secretly breed within us the lie that our suffering is not worth the time it will take to serve its purpose. Rather than developing healthy approaches to treating our wounds, processing our losses and letting our tears fall where and when they may, we call upon culturally acceptable modes of anesthetizing ourselves, tritely called "coping mechanisms," to alleviate sadness and fear. Such methodology includes the rapidly rising use of vigorously promoted prescription drugs as the protocol for dealing with all kinds of issues regardless of the underlying cause.

According to the Center for Disease Control (CDC) benzodiazepines (aka "benzos") were involved in 31 percent of the opioid-analgesic poisoning deaths in 2011. [65] In addition to names like Valium, Ativan and Klonopin, among this class of medications is the fast-acting anti-anxiety pill, Xanax. In 2012, 49.2 million prescriptions were written for the generic form of this drug (Alprazolam) making it the 13th most commonly sold medication. [66] Two-thirds of the prescriptions that were written were done so for women. Consequently, the increased popularity and subsequent addiction rates of this drug among women have become an issue in need of immediate attention. Not surprising in a world where the lines between true panic disorders that may require medical intervention and everyday stress have become blurred, one of my "thirty something" students enlightened me on the frequent "popping of happy pills" by employees in her former department at a major corporation. On a larger scale, the number of trips to the emergency room nationwide from the misuse and abuse of Alprazolam more than doubled from 57,419 to 124,902 during the years 2005 to 2010. [67]

While I have known women who have been seriously and dangerously depressed and have sought out immediate intervention, which included doctor-prescribed drugs as part of their overall plan of getting better, I also have friends who succumbed to taking antidepressants because of the tremendous pressure put on them to do so. In some cases, medications like Paxil and Prozac actually made them feel worse and included thoughts of suicide—a possible side effect of these drugs. [68] Referring back to an exceptionally challenging time in her life, one woman who wanted professional help without drugs to address the emotional pain she was experiencing during the loss of her marriage told me the following:

> *I had every reason to be depressed going through my divorce. I was told by my (primary care) doctor that the serotonin in my brain had been depleted, and that I needed to put it back temporarily with an anti-depressant (Paxil). I was very apprehensive and afraid to take anything that affects the brain. He confirmed with me that I would only be on it temporarily and would not feel any different, just have the energy to move on. I was never told that I would also need to be on a sleep aid (Xanax, Ambien, etc.) because you can't sleep on them. The only thing Paxil did for me was stopped me from crying and having any emotions at all. I was FLAT. I didn't think things through, nor did I care about anything. I desperately wanted to get off because of all the health side effects (stomach problems, throat problems, etc.), and I didn't like not having any emotions. When I tried to wean off Paxil and went to the doctor because of the horrible withdrawals, he asked me: "What do you want me to do about it?" (Soon after) the Lord led me to a Christian psychologist who helped me wean off the drug.*

For more on this issue, I turned to Maryann Folco, a beautiful Christian friend who holds a master's degree in counseling and is a licensed drug and alcohol counselor (LPC and LCADC). She is quick to point out that part of the problem is that rather than differentiating between legitimate chemical imbalances that may require medicine and dealing with everyday problems we have evolved into a pill-popping culture wherein we are told, "You're feeling blue? Take this; you'll feel better." Indeed, as Folco points out, decades-old songs like the Rolling Stones' *Mother's Little Helper* ring true today as so many women turn to the pill bottle to deal with the stresses of everyday life. Unfortunately, as Folco notes, this mentality apart from a true effort to address the root of the pain "doesn't get us better; it gets us numb."

Worth noting is that the increased manner in which potentially harmful drugs are prescribed these days is not confined to any one area of pain. An October 2013 segment of the *CBS Evening News* depicted a heart-wrenching story of returning war veterans receiving lethal amounts of pain medication by Veterans Affairs hospitals including the highly addictive drug Oxycodone. Sadly, as referenced in an introduction by the anchor Scott Pelley, CBS learned of "case after case of veterans who've died after following doctor's orders." During an interview conducted by reporter Jim Axelrod regarding a Congressional investigation into these findings, Veterans' Affairs Committee Chair Congressman Jeff Miller stated, "Unfortunately it has become a routine way of dealing with our veterans is to give them a prescription—they walk out the door with their medications, and masking the pain only temporarily takes it away." Following through on these comments, Axelrod noted that such practice "does not treat the underlying cause," to which Miller responded, "No, and it's the underlying cause that absolutely has to be treated." [69]

As with the trite words that are doled-out in an effort to move someone on and out of their present and no-doubt painful state, swallowing a pill just to make the issue go away without careful thought to the consequences is not a credible antidote. Sadly, in our world's desperate and sometimes even well-intended attempts to bypass that which is hard we ultimately do little more than build inventory, stockpiling pain upon pain that eventually will manifest itself one way or another, sometimes in ways that can be emotionally and physically devastating. A balloon can only hold so much air before it pops.

In an age where medications are so vigorously marketed to us as the "cure-all" for what ails us (just count how many commercials for prescription drugs you see in one airing of the evening news), how can ordinary, untrained people know if their tears are a normal biological response to the intensity of their circumstance or if they are suffering from a serious form of depression that requires treatment? Succinctly put *how do we know if our crying is healthy?*

In their book, *New Light on Depression: Help, Hope, and Answers for the Depressed and Those Who Love Them,* authors

David B. Biebel (who holds the Doctor of Ministry in Personal Wholeness) and Harold G. Koenig (board certified in several areas of psychiatry and geriatric medicine) explain that because of its complexity, "nailing down a definition of depression is like trying to nail psychological Jell-O to a wall." [70] Because of this, they "prefer to keep it simple" and describe depression as "a state of existence (not a state of mind) marked by a sense of being pressed down, weighed down or burdened, which affects a person physically, mentally, spiritually and relationally." Symptoms of this state may include relationship problems (withdrawal), irritability, excessive or inadequate amounts of sleep, fear of losing one's mind, low energy, decreased sexual desire, problems remembering and thinking, over or under eating and feelings of worthlessness. Noting that a person may be heading toward major depression, Drs. Biebel and Koenig recommend a professional evaluation if several of these characteristics are present. At that point, counselors, psychologists and psychiatrists trained to recognize the signs and stages of depression can determine if treatment including talk therapy is warranted. [71]

One instance where an expert assessment was critical was in the case of my friend Denise who says she has had symptoms of depression from the time she was 12 years old: "In the beginning, I was always able to manage it by doing enough so people would think I was o.k. I would deliberately seek out opportunities where I was visible such as through the performing arts. This gave others the impression that I was fine. Also, 'partying' gave the 'illusion of happiness.'"

Despite her struggles over the years, Denise went to college, graduated and became a registered nurse. Ultimately the added intensity of working with terminally ill patients (hospice) would make it impossible for her to mask her escalating symptoms of depression which at its worst included an inability to stop crying. Sleep loss, agitation and the inability to focus and complete her paperwork would eventually morph into a state of hopelessness with no end in sight and a desire to die. Even though Denise thought focusing on someone else's problems would allow her to continue to ignore her own, she now recognizes, "It is hard to look in the face of death and not be affected by it at some level and usually on a deeper level than you realize."

Eventually other nurses began to observe Denise's symptoms and suggested she seek out counseling. In doing so, the counselor saw that Denise was suffering from a clear emotional disorder and probable chemical imbalance and connected her with a psychologist who diagnosed her with posttraumatic stress disorder, anxiety and depression. Because she had experienced episodes of mania, Denise was also deemed bipolar. Her treatment included trying out a variety of medications including the antidepressants Prozac, Paxil and Wellbutrin as well as sedatives, sleeping medications and antianxiety drugs. As a nurse Denise realizes the difficulty of the field of psychiatry in trying to find the right medicine: "It's not like a broken bone where you just take an x-ray."

Shortly after beginning treatment, Denise found it necessary to be admitted for a month to an inpatient psychiatry unit. Soon after her discharge from the hospital, Denise—who had accepted Christ when she was just a little girl—rededicated her life to the Lord, left nursing to pursue a degree in music (the field she always wanted) and now has been off medication for more than fifteen years. While she still faces the struggles of everyday life including a crisis or two along the way, she now knows to turn to the promises of God in emotionally difficult times rather than the dangerous addictions and coping mechanisms of days gone by. She came to recognize that *admitting she needed help and getting well was a journey.* Sometimes we, like Denise, just need some help in knowing where to begin.

In James 1:2-4 the writer by the same name speaks about the joy that can be ours through our trials as we begin to believe that it is through these times God is building in us the ability to "persevere" in our faith. It is what I like to think of as making us *hardy Christian stock.* In the sentences which follow these verses James shows us that we are not chided during times of trial for not having all the answers regarding our present circumstances. *Instead, we are encouraged*—as James points out—to turn toward a loving God who stands ready to help us know what to do:

If any of you lacks wisdom, he should ask God, who gives generously to all without finding fault, and it will be given. But when he asks, he must believe and not doubt, because he who doubts is like a wave of the sea, blown and tossed by the wind. [72]

The key to these verses is *to ask God and believe that He will answer* keeping in mind—as seen in the verses that proceed this—that most times God's wisdom comes by way of *a process* as part of His master plan to develop our perseverance by increasing our *faith.* As God has shown me, real faith is best defined as "believing God IS Who He says He IS!" Ultimately, it is this line of thinking, not our own efforts, that makes us *stable* or *steadfast in our minds regarding God's love for us no matter what!* James clearly knows this, warning us that it is *when we begin to doubt that God will do what He says He will do* (in this case, give wisdom) *that trouble sets in* causing us to become confused and unsettled, tossed around by the lies of the Enemy who is the author of doubt.

Though, as in Denise's case, resolution and healing may be a journey, we can trust God to give us wisdom and get us where He is leading us which is always into a place of hope! This does not come by "mustering up enough energy" to believe what God is saying, but rather it is a matter of *resting* in His truth as we wait for the winds of chaos to blow by.

With two decades in women's ministry and having lost one friend to suicide, I praise God for these truths as I recognize that, *yes, even mature Christian women who pray every day and read their Bibles are not immune to serious forms of depression.* Since the objective of Satan is to "rob, kill and destroy," [73] he will continually look for any sign of weakness in our lives—times in which we are tired, facing a crisis, loss or change—to try and capitalize on his desire to get us to doubt the promises of God. Such happens as we believe Satan's carefully crafted lies. As we believe the lies, we spiral downward as we are disconnected from the truth of God's love for us. We cave underneath the mountain of hopelessness and discouragement with which the Enemy will literary try and bury us. God knows this happens. Given that, it is important to realize that *just because a woman is battling depression does not mean she is a failure at her faith.* Instead, it is God's plan during these seasons to patently reinforce our need for Jesus—Who in the Book of Isaiah is called "Wonderful, Counselor." [74]

While we may not be able to change the nature of the circumstances that caused our present season of suffering, we can begin to believe in the love of God to bring us through remembering there is none safer with whom to cry. It is often in our darkest moments that the light of His love for us begins to shine forth in truly magnificent ways. This happens through the ministry of the Holy Spirit Who is called "the Counselor" and "the Spirit of Truth" [75] and lives inside of everyone who has truly trusted in Jesus for salvation.

In addition to the guidance provided for us by way of the Bible, the Holy Spirit very often uses the people who best know us to help us in our journey. With that said, it is important to recognize the danger of isolation. Clearly, because we were designed to live within communities, God never expected that we would be able to master all of our issues alone. Often He will use the wisdom and prayers of those *who love us and desire to see us be well* (the keys to finding the best help) as part of the process. For those who would turn inward toward drugs, alcohol or the Internet, my counselor friend Maryann Folco has said, "The problem with addictions is that they create distance between us and God which, as in the Garden of Eden, is always a clear goal of the one (Satan) who hates Him."

Accordingly, while I am a firm believer in *alone time* to regroup and draw near to God so He can speak to my heart, I also recognize how important it is to have a support system of tried-and-true prayer partners with whom I stay connected *who I know love me.* I realize—especially during exceptionally challenging times—that they will be available to help me sift through what's going on in my head. Even when they don't have all the answers, I can trust them to pray for guidance and direction for me. In my particular case, I am remarkably blessed that I have two female friends to whom I can turn for prayer who are professionally trained to recognize symptoms of depression. I also know a trustworthy Christian man who is a medical doctor who has always been there for me regarding any of my medical questions. *Along these lines, I would encourage any of you who are suffering in silence to reach out.* If you do not have a Godly friend to whom you can turn, start by believing that the Lord wants to give you wisdom in your time of need and refer to the resources in the back of this book. No matter how insignificant you may feel or intense your pain may be, you are part of God's master plan!

Having had her own struggles with postpartum depression following the birth of her first daughter—a journey that led her into her own relationship with Christ—Maryann Folco recognizes, "My road to Jesus happened through pain." Because she knows this at a deeply personal level, she encourages her clients in their desire to break free from substances and the fear of dealing with their emotional pains by helping them look past the mindset of a quick-fix and pointing them toward the opportunities awaiting them as they address their pain. "Rather than looking for immediate relief, we need to get comfortable with feeling uncomfortable. We might be in a place where we will be able to hear God."

CHAPTER SEVEN:

When Tears Won't Come

I truly believe that tears are a gift from God, a way of releasing pain when we go through trials of pain and sorrow. There was a period in my life as an adult when I had great difficulty crying. I would feel deep emotion inside, of sorrow or perhaps great frustration with the need to cry, but I could not. I knew that if I could just let go and weep, I would feel better. Finally, I began to pray and ask God to "give me tears" when I felt the need to cry. It didn't happen right away, but as I persisted in prayer, the time came and I was able to release my sorrow by crying, with tears.

Words of a friend after a miscarriage

In contrast to those who seek to avoid tears at all costs are those who simply are unable to cry. No doubt, there are a variety of reasons for this, some of which may be hormonal. Other times, as in the case of the woman in the last chapter whose tears dried up as a side effect of Paxil, medication can be a factor. In some situations, as with my friend who miscarried, we simply do not have answers. And while many of us typically connect crying with sadness some individuals experiencing specific kinds of clinical depression find that as their hope that their situation will change dries up so do their tears. As author Tom Lutz notes, "Fully detached and hopeless, they have lost the impetus to cry, because without desire there are no tears." [76]

With the last of these thoughts in mind comes a recognition that tears somehow carry with them the quiet hope that *someone is listening.* That someone cares. Even done in private—whether we are willing to admit it or not—tears have a way of letting us know that we are not alone; that perhaps God truly does exist and is quietly present in the process of pain.

At one point, Jennifer, who we talked about in the previous chapter, realized this. Believing she somehow "wished away" her newfound tears, Jennifer found herself pleading with God to bring them back:

> *Every sermon, every song, every touch from God prompted an outpouring of my soul. Eventually, the sensitivity offended me. I didn't like the emotion I allowed myself to feel because it humbled me and allowed me to become transparent in front of others. It was uncomfortable for me, and I wanted to run away from people again. Then God allowed a dry season to take place and soon I began to miss those tears. I recognized the gift He had*

given me and wanted to enjoy that gift, but was still afraid
of being hurt.

In Jennifer's case fear of being judged or manipulated caused her to return to the tearless life she had previously known. This time, however, it was with a deep recognition of what she had lost. Hindsight helped Jennifer to realize the beautiful healing and intimacy with God that quietly had been taking place in the process of addressing and surrendering her hurts. Like a seed unnoticed beneath the ground, tears were helping to bring into bloom a season of renewal and rebirth. Being real before God was setting her free. Ultimately, Jennifer discovered that humbling herself before God and seeking to please only Him had its rewards.

While Jennifer realized there is much blessing to be found for those who humble themselves through tears in the sight of the Lord, Scripture warns again and again against the antithesis of this truth: the sin of pride. Best defined as an all-out refusal to let the Holy Spirit work His truth in us, pride runs contrary to the intimacy that humility brings resulting in a disconnect from God. Often the doorkeeper for unresolved feelings of anger and resentment, pride posts a warning sign that says, "Keep out." Typically at its root is the all-too-familiar inability or downright refusal to *forgive.*

Whether directed toward a person (including oneself) or at God, unforgiveness is a fertile breeding ground for stress carrying with it serious consequences. Absent of the release that comes with honest tears, holding tightly to past offenses by refusing to let God into our wounds can result in the onset of a variety of physical and emotional illnesses including headaches, gastrointestinal problems, depression, anxiety and all kinds of fear. As I once heard someone say, "Unforgiveness is like swallowing rat poison and waiting for the rat to die." Succinctly stated, unforgiveness makes us sick.

Though there are many reasons why people in this fallen world become ill, including injury and genetic and environmental factors, Scripture speaks to the fact that some people become sick because of sin. Recognizing its significance, James 5 directly speaks to this issue:

> *Is any one of you sick? He should call the elders of the church to pray over him and anoint him with oil in the name of the Lord. And the prayer offered in faith will make the sick person well; the Lord will raise him up. If he has sinned, he will be forgiven. Therefore confess your sins to each other and pray for each other so that you may be healed.* [77]

Of particular interest concerning this passage is the phrase "confess your sins to each other" which specifically relates to sins that are committed against other people. Unforgiveness is one such sin that left unaddressed may result in illness.

Many years ago at a women's retreat, I had the opportunity to experience firsthand a situation like the one spoken of in James 5 when a woman asked me to pray for her because she was recently diagnosed with an autoimmune disease. In the process of getting ready to pray, I carefully asked her if there was any known sin she had not confessed. Almost immediately she told me that she was angry with her mother-her-law. After she admitted this, I prayed with her. Though I saw her quite a few times over the years during which she had other requests, I do not recall her ever again mentioning or asking for prayer for that illness.

Despite James 5 and the mountain of evidence contained in other parts of Scripture regarding the consequences of unforgiveness, some—even those who have been Christians for decades—downright refuse to forgive for they have falsely bought into the lie that if they extend forgiveness their offender will go free and justice will not be served. Like most problems in life that are based on a lie, this attitude is one that fails to align itself with the truth of Who God really is. If we actually believed that He will one day right the wrongs as He says He will (He is a God of justice), we would be quick to forgive as His Word calls us to do. God knows that we are not only hurting ourselves but others for whom He sent His Son to die. As John 3:17 tells us: *He did not send His Son into the world to condemn it, but to save it.* It is only as we are connected to this truth—realizing that God forgave us when we did not deserve it—that we in turn are prompted to remember the words of the *Lord's Prayer* contained in Luke 11:4: "Forgive us our sins as we forgive those who sin against us." Truly, we can only be forgiven to the extent that we forgive others. To harbor an offense against someone else once God convicts us to forgive is to have sin that remains unconfessed. And while holding tight to unforgiveness will not deprive us of spending eternity with God if we have truly accepted Christ as our Savior, failure to heed God's Word and the conviction of His Holy Spirit will not only affect our physical bodies but deprive us of extraordinary communion with a God who loves us and desires for us to experience "the exceedingly, abundantly more than we could ask or imagine," [78] or as I like to put it *more of Him.*

With this in mind, it is important to realize that one can only forgive to the extent that one knows that one is forgiven. Such an understanding begins and ends with the fact that Jesus Christ truly paid the full ransom for all sin at Calvary's cross. Scripture calls Jesus "a man of sorrows, and familiar with suffering (who) took up our infirmities and carried our sorrows. Pierced for our transgressions, He was crushed for our iniquities; the punishment that brought us peace was upon Him, and by His wounds we are healed." [79] Therefore, "everyone who believes in Him receives forgiveness of sins through His Name." [80] Because of this we who have been forgiven much are called by God to do the same.

A new or renewed understanding of this truth can be exceptionally helpful to those recovering from loss. As Elizabeth Kubler Ross and David Kessler recognize in their book *On Grief and Grieving*, in which the five stages of loss are clearly defined, anger and resentment are commonplace in the process of grief. [81] As I have had to realize in more than one situation involving someone or something I lost, forgiving others and myself for what I could have done differently were mighty catalysts for moving me forward to a place of healing. Key to this was agreeing with God when He showed me it was time to let go of my anger by confessing my hurts to Him, allowing my tears to fall and then trusting that He would *work all things to my good* [82] even in the places where there had been injustice. Responding to God's truth not only gave me peace but drew me closer to Him.

It is important to know God realizes that when we are hurt and angry being obedient can be a struggle. The Bible is full of individuals who faced such issues. Two very clear "before and after" pictures concerning the struggle to align our wills with God's are found in the Psalms 73 and 32.

In Psalm 73, the writer wrestles to follow along in the ways of God as He sees the wicked prosper seemingly, unlike him, without suffering. Believing that the arrogant will continue to get away with their sin, the psalmist cries out, "Surely in vain have I kept my heart pure; in vain have I washed my hands in innocence. All day long I have been plagued; I have been punished every morning." [83] Several verses later, however, the psalmist shows he has become keenly aware of his mistake admitting, "When my heart was grieved and my spirit embittered, I was senseless and ignorant; I was a brute beast before you." [84] Ultimately, he finds solace as he comes into the presence of the Lord where he begins to remember God's promise that one day justice will be served as the wicked will be destroyed.

Psalm 32 is an on-point example of the physically and emotionally debilitating effects of unaddressed sin followed by the healing effects of confession. During his attempt to conceal his immoral actions in taking Bathsheba as his wife, King David tells us: "When I kept silent my bones wasted away…my strength was sapped as in the heat of summer until I acknowledged my sin to You, and did not cover up my iniquity." [85] In ultimately responding to the conviction of God, David tells us he received unconditional forgiveness. He, therefore, encourages us also to go to God in prayer with the knowledge that He will receive us.

In view of this, rather than alienate and push Him away, we can be assured that healing awaits those who would respond to God's call to confess sin, extend forgiveness to those who have hurt us and receive God's forgiveness for our sin in return. This doesn't mean that God just glosses over our hurts with some sort of spiritual paint job as if they never happened. God realizes that it is actually normal to be hurt and angry when we are wounded, especially in regard to loss. The key, however, is to take our feelings to a God Who stands ready to meet us in our pain rather than using them as a license for ongoing resentment, which can make us sick. Sometimes the starting point is honestly admitting to God that we are hurt and don't want to forgive. It's o.k. to tell Him this because as an all-knowing God He is already aware of our feelings. As King David realized, we really cannot hide. We need to tell God we need His help to forgive because trying to do this without Him rarely works because to release completely those who have offended us is dependent upon the work of the Holy Spirit. As part of the process of sanctification, only He can fix (not patch) that which is broken.

In the Introduction to her book *Do Yourself a Favor... FORGIVE*, author Joyce Meyer who was repeatedly and horrifically violated as a child says, "Unfortunately, we won't go through life and never get hurt, wounded or offended. Experience tells us that life is filled with injustices. However, we can be free from the pain of these wounds by letting them go and trusting God to be our Vindicator and bring justice into our lives." [86]

Accordingly, when we forgive we put God back into the equation. Instead of hostility, there is peace. As burdens are released we become lighter and free. Tears often flow, fears are quieted, striving ceases to be and healing, along with newfound intimacy with God, takes place.

CHAPTER EIGHT:

Crying with Hope:
Birthday Reflections from the Graveside

Did I not tell you that if you believed, you would see
the glory of God? (Jesus to Martha at the tomb of Lazarus)

John 11:40

For most of the years since I became a Christian, I have not been what you might call a "cemetery person." It was rare since my father's death in 1997 that I would go to his grave. Because he had given his life to Christ shortly before he died, I knew that even though his old body was in the ground my dad was in heaven with Jesus, and I would one day see him again. The same held true regarding my grandmother who died the following year. For me, visiting the cemetery seemed to make very little sense, and as the years went by I held to this thinking. That was until 2010 when I and the rest of my church found ourselves in the aftermath of a suicide.

As can be imaged, the initial responses to Donna's death were all over the place. Many rightfully tried to find comfort by looking to her decades-long commitment to the Gospel of Jesus Christ as indisputable evidence that she was in heaven. On the other extreme, those fueled by the doubt and bad theology that rears its ugly head in times of crisis began to question the authenticity of her faith falsely believing that she had somehow committed some sort of "unpardonable sin." [87] For a handful of people, our treasured Gospel based on faith in Jesus Christ alone suddenly gave way to the lie of a salvation that could be "earned"—the "anti-message" of the Christian faith.

For me, just coming to grips with what had really happened proved to be my most immediate challenge. It was at this point that I suddenly found myself becoming a "cemetery person." Slowly over time, God somehow used Donna's gravesite to help me come to terms with what had transpired as well as to impart some of the wisdom I would need to continue my own journey of following Jesus after such a terrible tragedy and, hopefully, help some women along the way.

Going to the cemetery helped to sink in the fact that Donna was no longer on this earth. Seeing her name on the gravestone slowly served to reinforce this point. While I still had questions regarding how all of this could have really happened, being at the cemetery helped move me out of the fog of denial and into a place of acceptance that she was gone. Her graveside also became a place where I would pray for her family, sometimes with her sister-in-law who is my close friend. On one occasion, a special time of worship led by the members of the women's ministry I oversee was held at this site to commemorate Donna's love of the Lord Jesus Christ.

Ten months after her death, I was experiencing an exceptionally bad birthday. With my daughter in school and my mind out of sorts with how I should spend my day, I found myself once again in the car headed toward the cemetery. Sitting on the ground in front of Donna's grave, I soon found myself overcome by grief and spiraling downward into a chasm so dark that it truly frightened me. It was that place that Satan takes us Christians when his lies momentarily trump the hope of eternity.

Realizing that I had been disconnected from the truth of His Word, the light of God's love suddenly and unexpectedly broke through my debilitated state-of-mind as He reminded me that *it was o.k. for me to grieve, but as a Christian grieving for another Christian I needed to grieve in hope.* As it turns out the very truth that had for years kept me from visiting the burial sites of those I loved was the catalyst by which God would bring my thoughts back into focus as I sat covered in tears at Donna's gravesite:

> *We do not grieve like the rest of men, who have no hope. We believe that Jesus died and rose again and so*

we believe that God will bring with Jesus those who have fallen asleep with Him. 1 Thessalonians 4:13-14.

While these Scriptures importantly affirm that, *yes, Christians do and should be allowed to grieve,* God dutifully used them to remind me that Donna was alive with Him, and I would one day see her again. In this same moment of deliverance, God also began to bring into focus His promise that this season would eventually come to an end and result in an even greater realization of the hope that the process of suffering done in the light of His love was intended to bring:

> *We rejoice in the hope of the glory of God. Not only so, but we also rejoice in our sufferings, because we know that suffering produces perseverance, perseverance, character and character, hope. And hope does not disappoint us, because God has poured out his love into our hearts by the Holy Spirit, whom he has given us.* Romans 5:3-5

Having spent nearly a year leading a Bible study on the subject of hope, I have learned that the true hope spoken of in these passages really isn't some pie-in-the-sky form of wishful thinking. A repetitive theme throughout the Book of Romans, the word *hope* as it is used here carries with it *the intent of assurance.* Moreover, in Romans 15:13 God is called *the God of hope,* which consistent with its original Greek meaning tells us *God is not merely the subject, but the Author of hope.* [88] Hope, therefore is not just a "thing," but a *Person*. That Person is Jesus Christ.

Since the primary role of the Holy Spirit is to bear witness to the unsurpassing act of love on Calvary's cross, the love "poured out into our hearts" in Romans 5 is none other than the love of Jesus. Through Him, even the most excruciating suffering will ultimately lend itself to a deeper knowledge of who we are in Him. Having died for us, Jesus is the Epitome of suffering turned to hope—the glory of Easter morning—Who cannot disappoint. To grieve or suffer, therefore, without the presence of hope is to grieve without the knowledge of the love of Jesus clearly in sight.

Yes, tears would come as I processed the loss of my friend, but it was God's intention that they should fall in the context of His truth. His Word was the only way any of this would ever make any sense. Though Satan had temporarily blinded me to what I knew to be true, the light of the love of Jesus Christ broke through leading me back into the fold where I belong. In doing so I saw that for the Christian, no matter what our individual grief looks like, loss can only be rightfully processed in the light of eternity lest we give way to the lie of despair. It was almost as if God was saying, "Yes, Catherine, grieve, but GRIEVE FORWARD with and toward Me!"

For those sadly wrestling with the lie that the manner in which a believer dies can somehow invalidate that person's salvation, Scripture has this to say:

Who will bring any charge against those whom God has chosen? It is God Who justifies. Who is he that condemns? Christ Jesus, who died—more than that, who was raised to life—is at the right hand of God and is also interceding for us. Who shall separate us from the love of Christ? Shall trouble or hardship or persecution or famine or nakedness or danger or sword? No, in all these things we are more than conquerors through Him Who loved us. For I am convinced that neither death nor life, neither angels nor demons, neither the present nor the future, nor any powers, neither height nor depth, nor anything else in all creation will be able to separate us from the love of God that is in Christ Jesus our Lord. Romans 8:33-35, 37-39

Frequently, Christians sum up these verses with the *New Living Translation* of verse 39 which says "*Nothing* can separate us from the love of God that is in Christ Jesus." Nothing. Zero. Zilch. Not even suicide. Yes, it was sin outside of the will of God but an even bigger sin would be to say that the precious blood of Jesus is insufficient in its ability to cover something up in the life of one surrendered to Him. To believe such a thing would put an emphasis back on "works"—what we can do to earn our way into heaven—rather than the truth of Christ's sacrifice on Calvary's cross as the once-and-for-all payment for our sins. To say that His blood is inadequate to cover *all* sin is to oppose the sufficiency of His Word. In His book The Glorious Journey, Pastor Charles Stanley furthers this point:

> *Fortunately for all of us, God's grace is without prejudice. Whoever believes will be saved. Nowhere in the Bible does God compartmentalize sin and reserve grace only for those who commit "acceptable" sins. There is no such thing. Does God forgive suicide? Yes, He does.* [89]

Scripture enforces this truth by calling our salvation *a seal*, a mark of ownership that is absolutely irrevocable:

> *Now it is God who makes both us and you stand firm in Christ. He anointed us, set his seal of ownership on us, and put his Spirit in our hearts as a deposit, guaranteeing what is to come.* 2 Corinthians 1:21-23

> *And you also were included in Christ when you heard the message of truth, the gospel of your salvation. When you believed, you were marked in him with a seal, the promised Holy Spirit, who is a deposit guaranteeing our inheritance until the redemption of those who are God's possession—to the praise of his glory.* Ephesians 1:13-14

> *And do not grieve the Holy Spirit of God, with whom you were sealed for the day of redemption.* Ephesians 4:30

Though our salvation is not a license to do as we please [90] (a true Christian may struggle with sin, but seeks to live a life pleasing to God), the Greek words for *seal* as both a noun and a verb denote ownership, security and permanency: that which is fixed and certain by God, *the persons to be sealed being secured from destruction and marked for reward.* [91] Christ settled it. The ransom for our sins has been "paid in full." [92]

Because of this Christians can approach the death of *all* those who have died in Christ from the vantage point that our separation from them is temporary. While processing the loss of those we love is far from the easiest of tasks, aligning ourselves with the truth of what *God has to say* about these situations enables us to *grieve forward.* Slowly and certainly as we allow the Holy Spirit to draw us into truth, we, like Martha at the grave of her brother, will begin to see the promise of the glory of God as the real hope attached to the Gospel. As it does we will come to grasp the very special words of Jesus to all who would follow after Him: *Blessed are they who mourn: for they shall be comforted."* [93]

CHAPTER NINE:

Can You Hear Me Now?: How Real Men Can Listen, Learn and Love Through Real Tears

In bitterness of soul Hannah wept much and prayed to the LORD. And she made a vow saying, "O LORD Almighty, if you will only look upon your servant's misery and remember me, and not forget your servant but give her a son, then I will give him to the LORD for all the days of his life." And as she kept on praying to the LORD, Eli (the priest) observed her mouth. Hannah was praying in her heart, and her lips were moving, but her voice was not heard. Eli thought she was drunk and said to her, "How long will you keep on getting drunk? Get rid of your wine." "Not so, my lord," Hannah replied. "I am a woman who is deeply troubled. I have not been drinking wine or beer; I was pouring out my soul to the LORD. Do not take your servant for a wicked women; I have been praying here out of my great anguish and grief."

1 Samuel 1:10-16

The story of Hannah and Eli is a classic case of a guy just not getting it. While his intentions were probably good (drunkenness indeed leads to trouble and must be stopped at all costs!), Eli not only totally misjudged the reason for Hannah's tears but his blunt response came without even asking her why she was crying. His solution was to "fix things" and in doing so he completely missed out on the fact that Hannah's tears were a result of the pain common in the heart of a woman unable to conceive.

Centuries later, regardless of the circumstances that trigger it, the age-old dilemma of seemingly inappropriate responses by men to the tears of women continues to exist as crying women tell their counselors, friends and pastors that their husbands just don't get it.

"It's that *man brain*," one of my friends once told me. "They just don't think like we do." And, while there are a variety of reasons why men often respond differently than women, science indicates that my friend and her "man brain" concept have merit.

Dr. Louann Brizendine, a Yale University trained neuropsychiatrist and author of the books *The Female Brain*[94] and *The Male Brain* points out, "We now know that the emotional processing in the male and female brain is different."[95] Specifically, Dr. Brizendine explains that while both male and female brains contain the emotional systems known as the mirror-neuron system (MNS) and the temporal-parietal junction (TPJ), the MNS is larger and more active in women while the TPJ appears more dominate in men. Notably, the MSN more closely associated with women is an *emotional* empathy system which relies on facial expressions and tone-of-voice. On the other hand, the more male TPJ is a *cognitive* empathy system which gravitates toward a "just fix-it" solution. [96] Accordingly, while a man's tone-of-voice or expression might say to a MSN engaged woman, "He doesn't understand me," TPJ dominated men are frequently confused as they believe their "fix-it for her fast" response is evidence that they are genuinely trying to help. Often perplexed by what they deem as a "way too emotional reaction," men like Professor Henry Higgins in the musical *My Fair Lady* scratch their heads in response to teary women desperately trying to figure out why they don't respond to situations like they do.

Though Professor Higgins may have benefited from a lesson in contemporary science regarding the emotional workings of the male and female brains, this explanation is but one part of the issue. Together with this scientific basis, generations of cultural and societal influences regarding appropriate and acceptable gender-specific behaviors also account for much of the disparity between men and women particularly in regard to tears.

While it is good for men to understand that women are simply more biologically designed for tears and should be granted the freedom to cry when needed, God no doubt proved when He gave men lacrimal systems that emotional tears were intended to have a place in their lives as well. Running contrary to this truth, however, are the countless number of men who have been raised to believe "real men don't cry" or that "crying is a sign of weakness." Because of such false teachings, men often grow up under the pressure to suppress emotional tears. Consequently, in addition to developing the kind of problems that arise in the absence of a healthy process to deal with emotional pain and suffering, men into whose heads such erroneous information has been beaten (sometimes literally) run the risk of developing rigid, impatient, and at times contemptible, attitudes toward tears which may culminate in harsh and—at its extreme—abusive behaviors toward those in need of true support. Coupled with feelings of frustration in a situation in which he feels he has lost and must regain control, a man who has been conditioned to shut down tears may respond to the needs of a crying woman by telling her (less than nicely) to *knock it off*. When this response is directed toward a son or daughter, the cycle of abuse spins on absent of the truth that God purposefully gave the gift of emotional tears to men and women alike.

In addition to the examples of King David, Hezekiah, Job and Jeremiah referenced in Chapter Five of this book, the Apostle Paul who wrote the bulk of the New Testament lends credence to the truth regarding men and tears. Confident in his call to do so, Paul makes multiple records of his feelings expressed through tears:

> *I served the Lord with great humility and with tears and in the midst of severe testing by the plots of my Jewish opponents.* Acts 20:19

> *So be on your guard! Remember that for three years I never stopped warning each of you night and day with tears.* Acts 20:31

> *For I wrote you out of great distress and anguish of heart and with many tears, not to grieve you but to let you know the depth of my love for you.* 2 Corinthians 2:4

> *For, as I have often told you before and now tell you again even with tears, many live as enemies of the cross of Christ.* Philippians 3:18

Worth noting in regard to these passages is that *Paul was not exactly what one would call an emotionally weak man.* Having been imprisoned more than once for his faith, the true events of Paul's life depicted in the book of 2 Corinthians (which doesn't even include the time he was bitten by a poisonous snake) are "the stuff" from which modern-day gladiator movies are made:

> *Three times I was beaten with rods, once I was pelted with stones, three times I was shipwrecked, I spent a night and a day in the open sea, I have been constantly*

on the move. I have been in danger from rivers, in danger from bandits, in danger from my fellow Jews, in danger from Gentiles; in danger in the city, in danger in the country, in danger at sea; and in danger from false believers. 2 Corinthians 11:24-26

Notably, Paul did not put himself in these situations just to prove how *manly* he was. Rather, as the verses referenced earlier indicate, he found himself beaten, in danger and ultimately moved to tears because of the heartfelt pain that often accompanies *true love.* Having realized for himself the mercy and grace of a Savior who had come on a mission to deliver the world from sin and suffering, Paul's tears are not a sign of weakness but of *strength* from one who can ultimately understand the loss that looms large for those who remain outside the knowledge of salvation through the sacrificial love of Jesus Christ.

In his book *The Language of Tears,* Jeffrey A. Kottler, who identifies himself as "a therapist, an educator, supervisor of therapists and student of tears," recognizes the challenges of gender-specific expectations in regard to crying. [97] Cutting through the male/female stereotypes frequently assigned to tears, Kottler notes:

> *Crying is a language of really talking... It represents not only an attempt to say something but a plea for a particular response that involves both the head and*

the heart… it is not simply misplaced aggression, nor is it anger turned inward; it is the statement by someone of the depth and strength of the feelings. It is a sincere plea for understanding." [98]

No doubt in his passion for the Gospel, the tears of the Apostle Paul epitomize such a plea. Together with this truth, Paul's words carry with them a way out for men long held captive to emotional pain. Truly, healing and release from the power of decades-old lies await those men who would allow the ever-revealing ministry of the Holy Spirit to align their hearts with God's way of thinking regarding tears. Such a miraculous change in light of God's Word is what Scripture calls "being transformed by the renewing of our minds" [99] as we no longer hold tight to the world's way of thinking. Like a waterfall, the power of the past and the lies that fuel it come cascading down, sometimes in the form of tears. Yes, even for men, it really is o.k. As Dr. Frey notes in his research on crying:

I think many people need to learn that it is OK to cry and that they do not have to be strong all the time. One man told his therapist that he was afraid to let go and cry because he was afraid he would never stop. He and many others need to learn that they will not have a nervous breakdown if they totally let go and cry and sob. [100]

In addition to the individual freedom that comes forth in the light of truth, something even more amazing starts to happen as men and women alike begin to embrace God's true intention regarding tears. Slowly, suffering gives way to hope concerning the division between the anatomy of the male and female brains that seemed impossible to bridge. Transcending all biological, cultural and language barriers, the Holy Spirit uses the power of truth to bring men and women into a place of incredible unity which notably is God's ultimate goal regarding His church so that our lives will be a magnet for others in need of the freedom only He can provide. Such was one of the final prayers of Jesus before His long walk down Calvary's road:

> *I pray also for those who will believe in me...that all of them may be one, Father, just as you are in me and I am in you. May they also be in us so that the world may believe that you have sent me. I have given them the glory that you gave me, that they may be one as we are one—I in them and you in me—so that they may be brought to complete unity. Then the world will know that you sent me and have loved them even as you have loved me.* John 17:20-23

Despite the sin of this world and the barriers it creates, each ounce of truth—tiny though it may seem at the time—imparted through the ministry of the Holy Spirit to those who have trusted in Christ has the capacity to bring forth a unity beyond anything we as humans can do no matter how well intended and sought out our intentions may be. *Truly, what is impossible for man is possible for God.* [101] Where marriages are concerned—the institution that was meant to be the ultimate reflection of Jesus' relationship to the church—the possibility of mutual understanding beyond measure springs into life between a man and woman. Indeed, God is glorified as men and women begin to think alike as they focus on that which is true. Returning once again to the words of the Apostle Paul—words that became the guiding theme for my own wedding and the marriage that resulted—we are told:

> *Make my joy complete by being like-minded, having the same love, being one in spirit and purpose.* Philippians 2:2

That sameness in love, in spirit and in purpose is found as we allow the Holy Spirit to replace our age-old and worthless notions of long ago with the truth concerning God's beautiful design of that which He created as male and female. In doing so, we will find a God Who not only has given us permission to cry, but encourages us to bring our tears to Him that He might meet us in our time of need. Such an understanding is one that ultimately comes into focus in the story of Hannah and Eli.

Perhaps because she understood the release that awaited her after honestly pouring out her heart through tears to a God she knew loved and cared for her, Hannah notably did not respond defensively or argumentatively to Eli's unsolicited and hopelessly flawed reaction to her circumstance. Instead by merely presenting the true reason for her tears, Hannah helped Eli not only to listen but *believe her,* and rather than coming up with yet another "fix-it now" solution he began to think like-mindedly on the character of God concerning Hannah's situation. In doing so, Eli realized that her problem was one that only God could fix. Having now been brought into a place of compassion and understanding, Eli yet again addresses Hannah, but this time, he does so in an obvious spirit of agreement: "Go in peace, and may the God of Israel grant you what you have asked of Him." [102] Such a response communicated to Hannah: "I got it," and "I'm with you on this one." Herein lies the secret of loving women through their tears.

Realizing that God was the only One Who could fix that which was broken, Eli affirmed Hannah and trusted her heart to the One Who had created her and knew her best. Ultimately, Eli knew that God alone could meet all her needs. Rather than operating from a spirit of defeat in regard to his own inability to fix Hannah's problems, Eli instead received the blessing of strength that comes from knowing that God is lovingly in charge. *Such truth is undeniably empowering.* Knowing like Eli that honest tears poured out before the Lord are not in vain, men of today can likewise cease to believe they are failures, abandon their frustrations, and come to a greater intimacy in Christ by holding fast to God's truth concerning tears. In the end, men and women alike will truly be blessed beyond measure.

CHAPTER TEN:

The Smallest Yet Greatest Example

When Mary reached the place where Jesus was and saw him, she fell at his feet and said, "Lord, if you had been here, my brother would not have died." When Jesus saw her weeping, and the Jews who had come along with her also weeping, he was deeply moved in spirit and troubled. "Where have you laid him?" he asked. "Come and see, Lord," they replied. Jesus wept.

John 11:32-35

In the 11th chapter of the Gospel of John within the context of the story of Lazarus' death is what many Christians simply refer to as the shortest passage in the Bible: *Jesus wept.* Because it contains both a subject and a verb this tiny two word verse is by all means what my fourth grade teacher would call *a complete sentence*, a statement, in fact, very much warranting the use of a period. What makes this smallest of verses truly special, however, is the contrasting size of its message.

Four days after the death of His friend Lazarus, Jesus sets out to the town of Bethany to join the grieving family. Learning from her sister Martha that Jesus is indeed on His way and is asking for her, Mary runs out to meet Him closely followed by a group of Jewish mourners. Falling at His feet, Mary demonstrates both her faith and lack thereof by telling Jesus that had He arrived sooner rather than later, her "brother would not have died." Consequently, while Mary does recognize Jesus' ability to heal the sick her understanding of His power is contingent upon His physical presence while the sick person is still alive. Such a statement also suggests that Mary does not understand that in just a few moments Jesus would be raising her brother from the dead.

After taking notice of Mary's tears as well as the tears of the accompanying mourners, Jesus Himself also begins to cry. Important to this scene, however, is the ongoing reminder that *not all tears are the same*. In fact, a look at the original language in which this story was recorded shows that the tears of Jesus held a quality all their own.

Having first been written in Ancient Greek, the word *weeping* used twice in verse 33 in reference to Mary and those who accompanied her comes from the word *klaio* which is used to describe "any loud expression of grief, especially in mourning for the dead." Notably, in addition to the genuine grief exhibited by Mary and others in this group, *klaio* weeping is also used to describe the wailing of professional mourners who were customarily present in this culture and had no real relationship with the deceased. [103]

In contrast to this picture, the word *wept* in verse 35 used in regard to Jesus is taken from the Greek word *dakruo* which simply means "to shed tears." [104] And while Bible scholars, pastors and teachers throughout the years have offered a variety of noteworthy explanations concerning the specific manner in which *Jesus wept*, it is important to note that some of the discussion regarding this tiniest of verses lends itself to the specific role of tears in the process of suffering and loss.

While His move to emotion showed that He no doubt identified with the gravity of the situation at hand including the sting of death, the emotional pain of those He loved and, as many have suggested, the realization that His own death on Calvary's cross was drawing near, *as God in human form it was impossible for Jesus to wail and mourn in a manner that was utterly absent of the true meaning of hope.* To do so would be to defy the very mission for which He came which was to demonstrate God's glorious power over sin and death. In fact, several verses earlier in this same chapter just before this move to tears Jesus told Martha, "I am the resurrection and the life. He who believes in Me will live, even though he dies." [105] Accordingly, while *Jesus wept* over the reality of the immediate circumstances, He did so in light of the knowledge that He would be raising Lazarus from the dead foreshadowing His own death and resurrection and the promise of life everlasting for all who would trust in Him for their salvation. Succinctly speaking then, Jesus' tears were the perfect blend of the reality of loss and the hope poured out by the resurrection power of the Holy Spirit that would not disappoint. As Pastor John MacArthur writes, "While the Jews were correct in seeing Jesus' sorrow as evidence that he loved Lazarus, they were wrong to think that His tears reflected the same hopeless despair that they felt." [106]

In light of such knowledge, it is important to ponder why Jesus would bother to weep at all. Perhaps to some people taking the time to shed tears for a situation Jesus knew would end victoriously seemed rather pointless. Were not the tears of someone who could see beyond the present an unnecessary exercise in emotion? Why then didn't Jesus hold back the tears and shut down the process of suffering by assuring the crowd that all was well, shouting a couple of "Hallelujahs" and moving on to raise Lazarus from the dead? The answer to these questions lies within the character of a loving God Who makes time for suffering.

Rather than succumb to the trite answers sometimes doled-out in the awkwardness of the moment or a determination to move on and be done with it, *Jesus demonstrated the significance of identifying with and making time for suffering.* Accordingly, packed into the tiny verse of *Jesus wept* is a message that empowers all who would one day consider their personal right to linger in tears in seasons of pain this side of heaven. As God in human flesh, Jesus' example gave us the ultimate form of permission. In his piece titled "The Beautiful Tears," Makoto Fujimura writes:

> *If He came to Bethany to show His power and the fact that He is indeed the Messiah with the power to resurrect the dead, why did He not simply wave His "magic wand" to "solve the problem" of the death and illness of Lazarus? There would have been an immediate celebration, and all the tears would have been unnecessary. Tears are useless, even wasteful, if you possess the power to cause miracles. Instead, He made Himself vulnerable, stopped to feel the sting of death—to identify with frail humanity, who struggled to know hope.* [107]

In yet another commentary that considers this issue, Pastor Charles Stanley states, "Even though God knows the ultimate outcome of our suffering will be glorious, He still has compassion on us in the midst of our heartache." [108] Yes, resurrection would come, but Jesus demonstrated again and again that the authentic pain connected to emotional suffering this side of heaven should never be tritely passed by.

Notably, Jesus' example regarding tears and their God ordained connection to the process of suffering is not limited to His one example of *dakruo* weeping in the story of Lazarus. Perhaps the greatest testimony regarding such an issue is found during the agonizing hours Jesus spent in prayer in the Garden of Gethsemane just prior to His death.

Before heading out by Himself "just a stone's throw away," to pour out His heart to His Father in heaven [109] Jesus sets the intensity of the scene by confessing to his disciples that His "soul is overwhelmed with sorrow to the point of death." [110] Commonly accepted as a passage which speaks to this scene, Hebrews 5:7 paints a vivid picture of the suffering Jesus endured during those critical hours prior to His crucifixion:

> *During the days of Jesus' life on earth, He offered up prayers and petitions with loud cries and tears to the one who could save Him from death.*

By lingering long and hard in Gethsemane's Garden, Jesus not only made a true place for tears in the process of suffering, but bore witness to the presence of His Father God to Whom He prayed as One Who lingers with us during the darkest hours.

With these points in mind, Jesus' move to tears should shatter any notions that just because victory is in store suffering should be bypassed or dealt with quickly and lightly. Though believers in Christ do not grieve like those who have no hope,[111] we nonetheless are called to process our pain. As Bible commentator William MacDonald writes in regard to John 11, "The fact that Jesus wept in the presence of death shows it is not improper for Christians to weep when their loved ones are taken. However, Christians do not sorrow as others who have no hope." [112]

Like Jesus we too can do well in our example by not just jumping toward what we hope will be the "bells and whistles miracle of the moment," but rather by taking the time to deal with what is immediately before us and coming alongside the emotional pain of others through the ministry of tears. Such would be the mightiest of indications that we are tuned-in and listening. As nineteenth century pastor William M. Taylor notes in his work *The Miracles of Our Savior,* "the knowledge that he (Jesus) wept with the sisters in their time of sorrow gives us assurance that he feels with us in ours." [113] Even though and paradoxically *because He was God*, Jesus did not merely rush to Lazarus' or to His own grave "chin-up" just to move on and get it over with. Instead *Jesus wept*. Because of this, we too have been granted freedom to cry. God Himself is our truest model yet.

CHAPTER ELEVEN:
When We Linger

Tears are building up inside, trying hard to stay and hide,

So they'll not show how I feel and to others they'll reveal

Pain and vulnerability—welling up inside of me…

Now they're filling in my eyes and I don't feel very wise.

Can't control some simple tears any more than grief and fears.

Now I can't communicate and feel that I will suffocate.

Tears are now controlling me and I almost cannot see…

There they go; they have escaped, and they've ruined plans I'd shaped.

Suddenly those simple tears now are healing grief and fears.

Though the pain is very real, I am facing how I feel.

Tears have overflowed in streams, as I feared in recent dreams;

But I've found I did survive and I'm freer deep inside.

Thank you for your gift to me, washing eyes so I can see;

Letting tears and feelings blend—even tears can be a friend.[114]

Nancy Stoppelkamp

At the onset of this book, I told you about a special invitation I had received from God to linger with Him through the process of loss with the assurance that I would learn something about Him I had not previously known. I had no way of knowing through my tears at the time just how challenging His particular call to linger would be. Somehow in the exhaustion of my grief I had forgotten about the lengths to which Satan will go to try and disrupt God's plans for our lives.

While situations that involve suffering provide opportunities for us to draw near to God in truly intimate ways, the devil regularly and relentlessly uses the very same occasions to try and destroy our faith. Whether it is in the aftermath of a friend's suicide or some other form of personal loss, the primary way Satan sets out to fulfill his mission is through his ongoing attempts to use our pain as evidence that God simply is not good. Because of this what may have been easy for some of us to believe about the character of God just moments ago is suddenly challenged. And, what we may have thought were rock-solid promises from a good and loving God—particularly regarding His love and protection—now seem to make little sense.

Feeling deceived and tremendously disappointed, we doubt our ability to hear God at all. Such being the case, the Enemy takes his schemes to the next level by attempting to get us to doubt the point of picking up our Bibles at all: *why bother if our understanding of what we thought was true is all messed up?* It was in the midst of that sort of struggle that I found myself when God suddenly showed up and began to reveal to me that promised "something" about Him I had not previously known.

With the Enemy's lies ringing loudly in my ears, God brought to my mind a picture of Jesus on Calvary's cross. I watched as He hung there with outspread arms surrounded by a large group who attended His execution intent on mocking Him while He was in pain. Fueled by the notion that if Jesus really was who He claimed to be He wouldn't be allowed to suffer, this crowd hurled out insults that specifically challenged Jesus' identity as One belonging to and loved by God.

It was in this moment that God helped me to understand at a significantly deeper level the extent of the suffering Jesus endured for us. As if the physical pain of the nails and the agony of death on a cross (suffocation) were not enough, I now sensed more clearly the cruel weight of the verbal abuse thrust on Him by those who actually took pleasure in tormenting Him during His most trying hours. In the most incredible and unexpected way since the loss of my friend I came to know an almost indescribable intimacy—a connection with God at a level previously unknown—as I powerfully realized that not only had He seen every one of my tears but understood the depth of my pain because Jesus really had walked His own road of intense suffering long before me. And He did it so I—and each and every one of you—could know Him in a very real way, forever and ever.

As God met me in my distress and profoundly ministered to the broken pieces of my heart, I also sensed His call to let others—women like me who are experiencing their own personal path of pain and change—know just how deeply they are loved. Such is a call to be embraced because I see that while those of us who have trusted in Jesus for our salvation indeed have an understanding of His love as it relates to our eternal security many of the spiritual and emotional issues with which we struggle are a direct result of our unrealized ability to take hold of just how deep Calvary's love was intended to penetrate our lives. Because of this we often fail to attain the peace and assurance God desires for us in seasons of trial as we slowly begin to cave in to the lies of despair hurled down upon us by the "mockers" who challenge the truth of God's love for us. Unaware of the true root of our issue, we begin to find fault within ourselves. Rather than recognizing that we are in a spiritual battle, we instead start to believe that our inability to have "victory" over our circumstances lies within our inadequacy as a Christian. With this false thinking in mind, we attempt to battle our way out of our situation in ways that only end up leading us into exhaustion and feeling like failures.

As with the picture of Christ hanging on the cross in agony surrounded by a sea of mockers, the Enemy's strategy of adding insult to our personal injuries by causing us to doubt the love of God for us can ultimately seem more horrific than the initial loss that spurred on our season of pain. And while he absolutely cannot separate a true Christian "from the love of God that is in Christ Jesus," [115] Satan knows that if he can somehow convince us that God does not really love us and care about our suffering utterly catastrophic consequences can follow.

It is no great coincidence then that each of the four Gospel stories which tell of Jesus' crucifixion go beyond letting us know that He was killed on a cross. The suffering He endured for our sake is the greatest demonstration of love, and the fact that He was mocked while He hung in physical agony is an undeniable picture of One Who is capable of identifying with the challenges that arise in our own seasons of pain. And—unlike many of the circumstances that cause us to suffer—at the Father's directive, *Jesus signed up for this.* Though He Himself was sinless, He endured excruciating emotional and physical anguish to reverse the avalanche of loss that started in Genesis. In doing so, He placed a value on our lives that goes beyond measure. In the end, I began to see that while His pain would ultimately result in the greatest gain of all time for those who believe, Jesus did experience *loss* at Calvary's cross at a level greater than any other in all of history.

Through my tears and the process of moving me through suffering into hope, God was beginning to make clear to me that if we as women truly come to terms with the lengths to which Jesus went to demonstrate His love everything else regarding God's promises for us would start to fall into place. Notably, God began to reveal this to me at a time when I had thought my own grief had gotten old and I was tired of being sad. Feeling guilty about my state, I desperately wanted to "move on" the way I thought I was expected to. I suppose I could have turned to something other than God to deal with the sadness. However, somewhere along the way I suddenly realized that the reason I still felt this way was because God had not yet done in me what He wanted to do. If I would forgo the junk food of the "quick fix" to dull my pain, stop trying to fight my way out of my circumstances and *yield* to what He in His sovereignty was allowing with the belief that He loved me, the door to the Enemy's lies would be slammed shut. Yes, I would hurt, but instead of self-condemnation there would come a freedom in accepting that it was o.k. that my period of grief was longer than I (and others) would have liked. *Not only was it o.k. to cry but it was in fact part of God's ultimate plan to help make beauty out of the ashes.* [116] There was a purpose in my pain, and though the circumstances connected to my suffering were indeed tragic God intended to use them to get to the root of decades-old lies regarding my perception of His love for me that I didn't even know existed, the goal of which was to bring me into a more solid understating of both Who He is and who I am because of Him. At the end of all of this was a message of love for all women who may have been struggling with their identities in Christ.

Truly, God was making it clear that my friend's death and the heartache of those affected by it did not go unnoticed by Him. God had indeed seen our tears and was intent on responding by showing me there was hope awaiting those who would take the time to press into His purposes in the aftermath of such a tragedy. Rather than trying to suppress or battle our way out of our pain, there existed through the love of Christ the promise of being *lifted up and out*. There were times of refreshing to be had. My own cup would be filled so that it could spill over and nourish others. God had a plan, and I could trust that this season would run its course consistent with His intention to give me and others like me *more of Him*.

As a result, I sit here today with the hope of advancing God's desire to let women (and men) know that *Jesus loves you* is so much more than the bumper sticker the world has made it out to be. Not only did Jesus endure a physical agony at a level no other human has ever known as He took on the punishment for every sin anyone of us has ever committed, He did it in the midst of a crowd that was cheering on His execution with the twisted desire to separate Him from the truth of His identity and the Father's love for Him. Because of this Jesus demonstrated that your life—no matter how filled with physical or emotional suffering it may be—*is worth something*. Regardless of how inferior, unattractive, insignificant or defeated you may feel, Jesus' example says you were well worth the pain He endured. To Him, *you are beautiful.* Your life has value for through Him you were created with a purpose. He really does understand your suffering because He has been there. Yes, Jesus really loves you, and even if you can't see or feel Him He is here with you now waiting for you to come into the truth of His presence, and, if you need to, *to cry.*

The longer I live on this earth and the more I learn about the Christian life the more I become absolutely convinced that no matter the size of the situation we are facing, *the answer to all our problems comes back to the message of love found in the Gospel of Jesus Christ.* Contrary to what the devil would have us believe, salvation through the cross of Christ is not simply a onetime experience that we check-off on our Christian to-do lists that gives us the right to head out for a bathroom break when the Gospel is being shared during a church service. Instead, this Gospel should draw us back again and again in new and magnificent ways to the ultimate sacrifice of love that was made for us. *Absolutely nothing else in life has more power than believing in the depth of this love.* Yes, loss and suffering will come, but hope will arise through the love of Christ that has been "poured out into our hearts by the Holy Spirit who has been given to us" [117] in ways beyond "anything we could ever ask or imagine" [118] if we will just allow God to meet us in our pain.

In the seasons in which we feel the weakest and our prayers seem to do nothing more than hit the air and return unanswered, an amazing transformation is instead quietly taking place for those who would hold fast to God. While lingering in tears and processing emotional suffering takes time and can hurt pretty badly, Jesus demonstrated in Gethsemane's Garden that the God of love will strengthen us as we pour out our hearts to Him. *Because God is Who He says He is* and keeps His promise to *work all things to the good of those Who love Him*, the Enemy's attempts to shatter our faith by rubbing the salt of confusion and despair into our wounds instead result in an opportunity to know Christ more deeply in His suffering. *We can trust Him with our tears.*

As a woman overcome with sorrow, Hannah knew this about God, and her example of allowing her tears to flow before His throne should bring freedom to all of us with broken hearts in need of a good old-fashioned meltdown. In her online devotional entitled *Transformation Garden*, Dorothy Valcarcel—author of *When a Woman Meets Jesus*—tells us:

> *This is how Hannah came to her Father. She didn't hold back anything. She brought her grief and sorrow. Her tears and wailing... Filled with emotions that were overflowing and misunderstood by family, friends and clergy, Hannah came to her Father to pray. As she walked into His dwelling place of comfort and His haven of hope, she*

gave Him her grieving heart. So often I fear, in the most painful moments of our own lives, when our emotional state is out-of-control, just because those around us can't understand or don't want to handle the searing pain that finds it's expression in our tears, we unfortunately make the assumption God can't or won't want to deal with our sorrow either. Yet, at the moment of our most striking loss and shocking pain is when heaven's arms are opened widest to embrace us in a circle of hope and healing. [119]

For the men who may not yet be convinced that tears were intended to fulfill a role in their lives, Reverend Billy Graham recognizes:

> *I believe God gave us tear glands for a good reason and we should not be embarrassed to use them... Men especially should not see tears as a sign of weakness. In the Old Testament stout-hearted men "lifted up their voice and wept" (Job 2:12 KJV). Tears were not considered unmanly.* [120]

Consistent with Reverend Graham's thoughts and contrary to some of the messages that falsely lead us to believe that Christianity holds with it the ability to paint a smile on our faces and march forth in victory immune to hardship, Jesus tells us that "in this world we will have trouble." [121] And while He goes on to finish this verse with the encouragement to "take heart" because He has "overcome the world," Jesus at no point calls us to forego the process of being real before God and the suffering that is in fact part of the Christian life. Instead through the promptings of the Holy Spirit, our troubles should serve to draw us ever closer into the truth of His love.

When nothing around me makes sense and none of the other promises God has given me seem like they are ever going to come to pass, I know I can always find relief from my burdens through tears in the safety of the presence of the One Who gave His very life to save me. Whether or not we can muster up enough strength to believe it, *God's love never fails.* [122] Gratefully that love is not contingent upon my ability to live life as a "super Christian," but on the finished work of Christ at Calvary's cross. As the events of that weekend which culminate in His resurrection ultimately show:

> *Weeping may endure for a night, but rejoicing comes in the morning.* Psalm 30:5b

With this picture in mind, we can rest assured that *crying is an appropriate and God ordained biological response to the losses of this life which hold at the end of them the promise of joy.* In seasons of pain, tears are a gift to be embraced, and to say "yes" to their plea to flow forth is to surrender into the purposes of a God "Who cannot disappoint."

While some may see those who accept the call to linger in tears as unhealthy, just the opposite is true. Though it may feel we are taking the long way out in this hurry-up-give-it-to-me-now world in which we live, God's call to process our pain will actually end up saving us time in the long run. Rather than giving way to the energy it takes to push our pain back into the dark, allowing God to lead us into the light through the process of suffering will help ensure that we will not have to spend a lifetime trying to keep our unresolved hurts at bay. Rightfully addressed through the ministry of the Holy Spirit, *wounds are healed.*

My friend Nancy Stoppelkamp who wrote the poem at the opening of this chapter is someone who intimately understands the value of lingering in tears. Like so many of us, Nancy is indeed no stranger to loss and suffering. During her first stay in a psychiatric hospital in 1969, doctors struggled to find the cause of Nancy's issues and initially misdiagnosed her with schizophrenia. Because her symptoms remained unresolved, Nancy would experience three more hospital stays and ultimately find herself in what she calls "a psychotic state and totally exhausted." Finally in 1981—in part because of information discovered by her husband—Nancy was diagnosed with bipolar disorder.

Adding to the weight of these struggles were the significant number of losses Nancy experienced along the way. In fact, she distinctly remembers that every time she went into the hospital someone she knew had either died or was in the process of dying. Because her family had moved, Nancy recalls the frustration of not being able to reach out through phone calls in response to some of these situations because at the time calling long distance was just too expensive. For Nancy, the greatest loss of all would come right around the time of her bipolar diagnosis when her sister Susan who had been battling cancer died at the age of 39. Reflecting on the closeness of their relationship and the significance of the loss, Nancy says, "Susan was my birthday present when I was four. She was not supposed to die before me."

Now decades later Nancy has come to recognize the important role tears fulfill in processing pain and is free to admit that she has done a lot of crying in her life. "In all of my loses," Nancy says, "if I had not been able to cry I don't think that I would have been able to make it through. My tears were absolutely essential."

As Nancy has come to realize, tears are a God-given gift meant to help us cleanse our way into emotional healing through the love of Jesus. Likewise for each of you beautiful women (and men) who have taken the time to read this book and maybe cried along the way, tears were intended to do the same for you. In light of this truth, may you embrace well and unashamedly the gift of tears knowing that your seasons of pain have not gone unnoticed by God, and in doing so know the unshakeable hope and depth of the love of the Lord Jesus Christ Who thought you were worth dying for.

CHAPTER TWELVE:

After the Flood

For forty days the flood kept coming on the earth,

and as the waters increased

they lifted the ark high above the earth.

The waters rose and increased greatly on the earth,

and the ark floated on the surface of the water.

Genesis 7:17-18

In the Old Testament Book of Genesis is a story that most of us are familiar with regardless of our religious background. It is the story of *Noah*. Because of his obedience and the contrasting sinfulness of man, Noah—at God's directive—found himself, his family and an ark-load of every kind of animal afloat amidst tremendous rainwaters. Surely it must have seemed that the rain would never end. *But it did*, and Noah and his family, along with all those animals, stepped off onto dry land.

As a sign that He would never again destroy all life with a flood, God gave the sign of the *rainbow* to Noah, his family and generations to come:

> *And God said, "This is the sign of the covenant I am making between me and you and every living creature with you, a covenant for all generations to come: I have set my rainbow in the clouds, and it will be the sign of the covenant between me and the earth. Whenever I bring clouds over the earth and the rainbow appears in the clouds, I will remember my covenant between me and you and all living creatures of every kind. Never again will the waters become a flood to destroy all life.* [123]

While many have come to know the connection of the rainbow to this particular passage, fewer, I believe, are aware that according to the New Testament Book of Revelation, it is non-other than this same symbol of covenant and promises kept that is associated with a life completely free of tears in the kingdom to come known more commonly as *heaven*.

As God would have it, somewhere along the way of the writing of this book—May 18, 2013 to be precise—the Lord saw it fit to take my own mother out of this world and into His presence. In short, she died, at least in the way the world perceives it. After a long period of both physical and emotional pain and suffering—a lifetime in fact—God called to His side a woman who had come to understand the hope through Jesus that does not disappoint. On that particular day, airing on the oversized television in her hospital room was an informational movie brought in by my sister on Hawaii—a destination my mother truly loved and to which she had hoped to travel one more time. Notably, right around the moment of mom's earthly death, during a segment on the island of Maui, a scene of a magnificent rainbow appeared on the screen. Almost immediately, the following Scripture reference from Jesus' revelation to John came flooding into my mind:

> *...there before me was a throne in heaven with someone sitting on it. And the One Who sat there had the appearance of jasper and carnelian. A rainbow, resembling an emerald, encircled the throne.* [124]

While mom did not make it to her beloved Hawaiian paradise one last time, God demonstrated to me in a truly tangible way just at the moment He took her to heaven that she instead had gone off to a place of extraordinary beauty far beyond that of any to which she could have ever traveled here on earth. And while the Book of Revelation goes on to give more details of what heaven is truly like, the greatest reason for its splendor lies within the verses which simply tell us *God is there.* Sitting on His throne as King of Kings and surrounded by the beauty of the rainbow, His presence signifies the end of our need to process pain, the receding of the floodwaters of our tears and the reality of promises kept:

For the Lamb at the center of the throne will be their shepherd; he will lead them to springs of living water. And God will wipe away every tear from their eyes. [125]

As in the story of Noah, the presence of the rainbow is a reminder that *God is a God Who keeps His word.* In the safety of His presence, the gift of tears will be no more as the suffering of this world will be completely washed away.

Though I made no effort to initiate a detailed investigation into the science behind the rainbow, I nonetheless found myself soon after my mother's death immersed in this subject when my daughter Molly decided to choose this topic for her science project. With an unmistakable love for rainbows, Molly has been known to go to great lengths to catch a glimpse of one including regularly taking the Lucite-like garbage can out of my bedroom and transforming it into a prism by capturing the morning light coming in from the window in our upstairs bathroom.

In helping Molly with her project, I learned that rainbows are formed when white light from the sun passes through water droplets like a prism and separates it into colors. The colors are then reflected off the back of the droplet and refracted again as they exit. I can't help but think that that is exactly what God does with us as the light of His Son shines through our lives and is reflected out into a world of hurting people in need of the knowledge of His love.

In addition to the giant poster board detailing facts connected to the rainbow, Molly was required to make a 3-D model to go along with her project. Since all of this needed to be completed in May, I unexpectedly found that I had a grand paper mache rainbow sitting on my dining room table right on the first anniversary of the loss of my mom. Working through the hands of my child, the God of the universe met me in my grief and once again used the symbol of the rainbow to remind me that my mom was with Him in His paradise free of pain.

With this in mind, it is comforting to know that in this world where hurting people are desperately looking for the assurance of an afterlife, God's Word plainly makes known to us the absolute reality of heaven. Unlike the dead-end paths down which emotionally vulnerable people are lured in seasons of loss and suffering, the Bible answers our questions about eternity through the certainty of salvation through the Lamb at the center of the throne Who is none other than Jesus Christ. Contrary to the messages of any other form of religion or spiritual practice, the central purpose of Jesus' death and resurrection is to *guarantee* an intimate and eternal relationship with God for those who believe. Such an assurance cannot be earned no matter how good we think we've been or how many religious activities we perform. It cannot be bought from those promising special blessings at a price nor can our questions about eternity be answered by someone claiming to have special powers regarding the afterlife. While it initially cost Jesus His life, eternity by grace through faith in Christ is now and always has been a *free gift* for all who would accept it. Ephesians 2:8-9 plainly tells us: *It is by grace you have been saved, through faith—and this is not from yourselves, it is the gift of God—not by works, so no one can boast.* No matter how anyone else tries to package it, Jesus gave His life freely, [126] simply because *God really does love us.*

These truths are particularly important to me because even though my mom practiced a form of religion and went to church, she spent almost all of her life outside of the absolute peace Jesus died to give her. Having had many opportunities to discuss spiritual things with her over the course of about 20 years, I watched with frustration as she continued to do things to earn acceptance by God and struggled to get past the pain of those who had hurt her including my father who died 16 years earlier of alcohol-related cirrhosis. Gratefully, as she began to ask God what *He wanted*, she came to know the unconditional and eternal love of Jesus Christ for her in a life-changing way. She was able to extend forgiveness and found release from much of the fear and depression with which she had struggled for most of life by trusting in the promises of God. Having been in and out of several comas during the last eight months of her earthly life, mom told me that God had been telling her during her first state of unconsciousness, "Don't be afraid."

Because of this and other intimate details in the days leading up to her passing, I am convinced that at the time of my mother's death she was not only ready to leave this earth but was truly longing to be with Jesus. Decades of suffering ultimately gave way to a real relationship with the One Who died to save her, and as it did a hope that cannot disappoint was born. For the first time in her life, a woman who had shed rivers of tears found acceptance—just as my dad did before his death—through the love of Christ, the ministry of the Holy Spirit and the peace that surpasses all understanding.

With her now safely in the arms of Jesus, I have in my possession a Bible I had given my mom many years ago that I wasn't sure she ever actually opened. In going through the pages, I found inside a small piece of paper with the words "Book of Acts Chapter 3 Verses 1-10" in her handwriting. Although it was possible that I did, I have no distinct memory of ever discussing these verses with my mom.

Not being able to recall off the top of my head what those verses talked about, I turned to that passage and found the title *Peter Heals the Crippled Beggar*. In this story a man crippled from birth was daily carried and placed in front of the temple gate to beg. Seeing Peter and John on their way to prayer, the beggar asked the two disciples for money. Instead Peter offered the beggar these life changing words:

> *Silver or gold I do not have, but what I have I give you. In the Name of Jesus Christ of Nazareth, walk.* [127]

The passage goes on to tell us:

Taking him by the right hand, he (Peter) helped him up, and instantly the man's feet and ankles became strong. He jumped to his feet and began to walk. Then he went with them into the temple courts, walking and jumping, and praising God. [128]

Through these verses that were somehow significant to her on her days on earth, I pictured my mom who had not been able to walk for the last eight months of her earthly life with a gorgeous smile on her face reaching out at the moment she left us to take the hand of Jesus and immediately leaping to her feet *walking and jumping and praising God.* Indeed for mom and all those who said "yes" to the message of love through the Gospel of Jesus Christ, ultimate healing had occurred as suffering gave way to permanent joy and celebration.

Although the flood of tears through the process of loss will come to us this side of heaven, the rainbow serves to remind us that God is a God Who keeps His promises. Through Jesus He has provided an Ark through which we in our suffering can rest secure floating on the surface of the water of His love poured out at Calvary's cross. Knowing well that *nothing* can separate us from Him, we can be sure that our suffering will end with the promise of heaven and everlasting joy:

He will swallow up death forever. The Sovereign Lord will wipe away the tears from all faces. Isaiah 25:8

In Closing:

A Word to Church Leaders

During my years as a grief counselor, I have always stressed that grief is a process that moves at its own pace. It is not confined to a specific length or time frame nor does it take on a defined behavior but is rather very individual in each person. What may take months to work through in one person may take several years in another person's life. Tears in this grief situation validate the pain one is going through and are an expression and release of that pain.

Ann Marie Klein, BSN, RN, NP

Jesus was and today continues to be the most authentic Person Who ever stepped foot on this earth. After all, He is God, the One through Whom all things, including us, were created. Therefore, our goal in the process of sanctification should always be to become more like Him by yielding to the nudge and power of the Holy Spirit Who lives in all of us Who truly call Him our Lord. Part of this process not only includes heeding the words of Romans 5:3-5 as a church, but outwardly embracing God's truth concerning the suffering that follows any kind of loss by coming alongside those we—as good, gentle and *patient* shepherds—are called to lead. A necessary condition to this directive is that we lay down our fears of appearing unhealthy to the world we are longing to draw through our church doors and coming to a true understanding that *real* is not only what people are looking for, but need. This doesn't simply come by embracing the techniques of the latest/greatest "seeker sensitive" seminar or by trading-in our best Sunday clothes for skinny jeans and a t-shirt but by stripping away the "all-is-well" masks we sometimes put on in the hopes that people will like us. Rather than mistakenly worrying about what kind of witness our present crisis might be, we must see that efforts to ignore, dress or cover it up amount to little more than the sin of denial, no matter how well-intended our desire to keep moving forward and put this behind us may be. Such a strategy never works. Like any other unresolved issue in life, the consequences will simply pop up someplace else.

In the church's quest to be a happy, fun and hip place where people want to come, we must not ignore the cries of individuals who in their suffering are begging us to allow our previously mapped out plans to be interrupted along the road as Jesus did. We must not be deceived into believing that our path to success and church growth is one marked by the world seeing us as strong, even after a major crisis occurs. Some of

Jesus' perceivably weakest moments did none other than point to the strength of the Father He was seeking to please. We must by way of ongoing prayers for sensitivity seek to lead minus the language of *Christianease* and a one-size-fits-all Scriptural bandage for the suffering. Both men and women must turn to the Word of God for guidance so we might rightfully come alongside one another in our pain.

For me, the personal invitation to linger with God in grief after a church crisis was an opportunity to be part of the solution in helping to shatter the stereotypes regarding what we as leaders are supposed to look like. The crisis facing us was so extraordinary that no matter how trained some of us were we were undeniably, directly and personally affected. On a personal level, *being real* required letting others see that I too was hurting and didn't have everything all figured out. Yes, hurting people were looking for leadership, but I came to see that part of that meant realizing afresh the leadership style of Jesus Who not only validated the pain and suffering of those around Him by giving them time but by also letting them see that He too suffered, and, yes, even cried. Such is the greatest living example and all the proof we as believers truly need to authenticate God's design of our bodies as one that includes the requisite that we sometimes bring forth tears. Indeed, our willingness to be this real in seasons of pain could be a powerful catalyst for those who need to know it is *safe* to let us know they are suffering. As one who has served as a worship leader for nearly two decades I can personally testify that people in their uncertainty often take their cues regarding appropriate church behavior by watching how the pastor sitting in the front row is responding. In the same way, we as leaders need to demonstrate that it is both safe and desirable to be real.

With this said, we realize again that part of being a leader is to actually *lead*, and, unfortunately, we sometimes confuse that with the need to be popular. We should resist the temptation to compromise truth for the sake of appearances because we fear we will look bad. *We should never compromise Jesus to be Jesus.* He suffered. He wept. He was never trite. We must, like Eli's assessment of Hannah, recognize that if we've simply gotten it wrong we need to make it right even if our initial intentions were good. Yes, leaders make mistakes. God in His love, mercy and compassion will not brand us as failures at the Christian-life if we simply cannot pick ourselves up and move forth "joyful" and "victorious in our faith." Such a response short-circuits the beautiful intention of suffering that results in true "perseverance, character and a hope that cannot disappoint." [129] Slowing down and saying "yes" to God's timetable allows us to hear the Holy Spirit and gives Him a remarkable opportunity to reveal the very model of a Savior Who embraced suffering for the sake of eternal hope. For reasons I will never completely understand this side of heaven, Jesus' example says we as people were worth dying for.

I believe that we both individually and collectively as a church body are given throughout our earthly lives the equivalent of the "little boy's lunch." Where this Gospel story is concerned, the contents of such a meal consisted of a few small fish, some bread and a willingness by one child to offer what he had been given to the Lord. After His seemingly wary apostolic leadership realized what they had been given to work with, our compassionate Jesus took it, did the miraculous and fed many. [130] Such a picture of surrender epitomizes the very act of Jesus at Calvary's cross: one life offered up to feed many.

In the case of my church, our lunch bag contained the aftermath of a suicide. It wasn't pretty or initially what you might call the kind of meal you'd be looking to serve given that we so often come to the table for junk food rather than the seemingly icky and hard-to-digest foods God knows we need. But realizing what we had been given and offering it to the Lord was an opportunity to feed many. It was a sad and rare opportunity to help hurting people feel comforted rather than condemned in moments of God ordained tears and to show the world that we as Christians are not made of plastic.

May the God of the hurting give us each discernment and courage as we embrace our God ordained gift of tears throughout the seasons of our earthly lives that we might in turn help a world that is suffering to do the same. Truly what we can expect in return is "a hope that cannot disappoint." [131]

Resources for Those Who Hurt:

If you are feeling suicidal, **tell someone**: call 911 or go to your nearest Emergency Room! Jesus truly does love you, and your life on earth has a purpose!

- *America's Keswick* (*Barbara's Place for Women* and *Colony of Mercy for Men*): New Jersey based retreat center hosting a variety of ministries targeted toward recovery including residential programs for men and women dealing with issues of addiction. For more information contact: *Barbara's Place for Women*: 848-227-4590; *Colony of Mercy for Men*: 800-453-7942 or visit America's Keswick at <u>www.americaskeswick.org</u>.

- *American Foundation for Suicide Prevention*: Dedicated to understanding and preventing suicide and hosting overnight walks bringing awareness to the issues of depression and suicide. For more information visit <u>www.afsp.org</u>.

- *GriefShare*: Offering Christian based grief recovery support groups. To find a group in your area, call 800-395-5755. International: 919-562-2112 or visit www.griefshare.org.

- *Joni and Friends*: Providing help for individuals and families dealing with the challenges of disabilities. Learn more at 818-707-5664 or www.joniandfriends.org.

- *Joyce Meyer Ministries*: Dedicated to sharing God's love and the life-changing message of the Bible with the world. Prayer support available Monday-Friday, 7 a.m.-4 p.m. (Central Time)at 1-866-349-3300 or by sending a request: www.joycemeyer.org/everydayanswers/requestprayer.aspx.

- *Mercy Multiplied*: Christian residential program with U.S. and international locations providing assistance for women ages 13-28 struggling with debilitating life-controlling issues. Learn more by calling 615-831-6987 or at www.mercymultiplied.com

- *Moriah Ministries*: New Jersey based ministry encouraging time out at the feet of Jesus through prayer, worship and teaching with annual retreats in New York State. Email info@realwomencry.org to learn more.

- *National Suicide Prevention Lifeline*: 1-800-273-TALK (1-800-273-8255); National Crisis Help Line: 1-800-SUICIDE (1-800-784-2433); (Para obtener asistencia en español llame al 1-888-628-9454).

- *National Council on Alcoholism and Drug Dependence* (NCADD): Providing support for those facing substance abuse addictions. Call 212-269-7797 or visit www.ncadd.org for more information.

- *Overcomers*: Christian recovery support groups for a variety of issues using the 12 step model. To find a group in your area, call 800-310-3001 or visit www.overcomersoutreach.org.

- *Teen Challenge*: Christian addiction recovery residential program offering assistance for both teens and adults. To find a local program call 417-581-2181 or visit www.teenchallengeusa.com.

Notes and References:

Introduction: *Understanding this Book: Why Should We Cry?*

[1] For more on the subject of tears and monasticism as well as the connection of tears to other experiences associated with religion, see Lutz, Tom, *Crying: The Natural & Cultural History of Tears*, W.W. Norton and Company, Inc. NY, NY, 1999, pp.46-47.

[2] 2 Corinthians 10:5b.

Chapter One: *Permission to Cry*

[3] Copyright 2011, *Sherwood Pictures Ministry*, Inc. Albany, GA; Copyright 2011, *Provident Films*, Franklin, TN. Used by permission.

[4] Ephesians 3:20.

[5] Fruitbearer Publishing, LLC, Georgetown, DE, 2014.

[6] For more information on *GriefShare* and to find a support group in your area, visit *GriefShare.org* or call 800-395-5755.

[7] Waters, pp.xvii.

[8] Ecclesiastes 3:1,4 NLT.

[9] "Weeping is exclusively human. As far as we know, no other animal produces emotional tears." Lutz, p.17.

Chapter Two: *Some of the Real Science Behind the Tears of Real Women*

[10] Bergman, Jerry, "The design of tears: an example of irreducible complexity," *Journal of Creation* 16(1):86-89, April 2002; creation.com/the-design-of-tears-an-example-of-irreducible-complexity. Used by permission.

[11] Lutz, pp.67-68.

[12] Ibid, p.68. These findings were originally reported in the *American Journal of Ophthalmology* following a study conducted by Dr. William H. Frey. For more on the study, see Frey, W.H. II, Desota-Johnson, D., Hoffman, C. and McCall, J.T. (1981) Am J Ophthalmol 92:559-567. "Effect of Stimulus on the Chemical Composition of Human Tears."

[13] Adapted from "Overflow Tearing in Infants," *American Academy of Ophthalmology*, San Francisco, CA, 2014. Used by permission.

[14] Lutz, p.67.

[15] Ibid.

[16] *American Academy of Ophthalmology.*

[17] Ibid.

[18] Frey, William H. II with Langseth, Muriel, *Crying: The Mystery of Tears*, Winston Press, Minneapolis, Minnesota, 1985, p.50.

[19] *Miller-Keane Encyclopedia and Dictionary of Medicine,* Nursing and Allied Health, Seventh Edition. 2003, Saunders, an imprint of Elsevier, Inc. 14 Jan. 2014, http://medical-dictionary.thefreedictionary.com/alacrima.

[20] Alacrima is also common in children suffering from *Riley Day Syndrome* (also known as *Familial Dysautonomia*) which Molly does not have. For more information on this visit www.familialdysautonomia.org.

Chapter Three: *Emotional Tears and the Female Body*

[21] Frey, p.71.

[22] Lutz, p.72.

[23] Ibid., p.76.

[24] Ibid., p.70.

[25] Ibid, p.91-92.

[26] nlm.nih.gov/medlineplus/hormones.html.

[27] Frey, p.48.

[28] nlm.nih.gov/medlineplus/hormones.html.

[29] Hypothyroidism. A.D.A.M., Inc. http://www.nlm.nih.gov/medlineplus/ency/article/000353.htm. Updated May 5, 2014. Accessed December 10, 2014

[30] Ibid.

[31] Lutz, p.91.

[32] Frey, p.48.

[33] Ibid. pp.48-49.

[34] Ibid. p.81.

[35] Correspondence with Dr. J.M. Arrunategui, M.D., FACOG.

[36] Frey, p.50.

[37] Ibid. pp.51-52.

[38] *American Society for Reproductive Medicine Fact Sheet* http://www.sart.org/uploadedFiles/ASRM_Content/ Resources/PatientResources/Fact_Sheets_and_Info_Booklets/ Prolactin_Excess.pdf used by permission.

[39] Correspondence with Dr. Frey, January 16, 2014. According to Dr. Frey, evidence regarding differences in male and female lacrimal glands was most clearly shown by Ann Cornell-Bell in an article she published in *Investigative Ophthalmology and Visual Science* (Volume 26, Issue 8, 1985, pp. 1170-1175).

[40] Dr. Frey indicated that this information was published in *Endocrinologica Folia*, "Hormonal control of the lacrimal gland extraorbitale in mice with pituitary dwarfism," Folia Endocrinol. 16,123, 1963.

[41] Ibid.

Chapter Four: *The Benefit of a Good Old-Fashioned Meltdown*

[42] Frey, p.42 and Fooladi, Marjaneh M., "The Healing Effects of Crying", *Holistic Nursing Practice*, November/December 2005, p.249.

[43] Frey pp.52,54 as reported in http://www.nytimes.com/2011/01/04/science/04qna.html?_r=1&.

[44] Frey, p.119-120.

[45] Frey, p.2.

[46] By way of telephone correspondence July 3, 2014.

[47] Lutz, pp.146-147.

[48] Tomas, Amelia, "Why a Sob Fest Makes You Feel Better–or Worse," http://www.nbcnews.com/id/28366779/#.UvwqbE0o7rc. ©2012 LiveScience.com. For more information see Rottenberg, J., Bylsma, L. M., & Vingerhoets, A. J. J. M. (2008). "Is Crying Beneficial?" *Current Directions in Psychological Science*, 17, 400-404.

[49] Fooladi, p.250.

[50] January 1976, pp.19-21 as adapted from Frey, p. 132.

[51] Volume 7(2), 1979, as found at http://psycnet.apa.org/psycinfo/1980-28379-001

Chapter Five: *How God Sees and Responds to Our Tears*

[52] Isaiah 49:16 tells us that our names are "engraved on the palms of (His) hands." Isaiah 43:1 tells us: "I have redeemed you; I have summoned you by name; you are mine."

[53] David C. Cook, Colorado Springs, CO, 2010, used with permission from the Joni and Friends International Disability Center, p.61

[54] Isaiah 40:26-38.

[55] Job 16:20.

[56] Proverbs 18:24.

[57] Romans 8:28 tells us: *And we know that in all things God works for the good of those who love Him, who have been called according to His purpose.*

[58] Genesis 3:15.

[59] http://www.answersingenesis.org/articles/2010/12/27/the-promise-that-was-made.

[60] Genesis 15:6 and Romans 4:3 tell us "Abraham believed God and it was credited to him as righteousness."

[61] Romans 8:28.

[62] Isaiah 61:1b-3.

Chapter Six: *We Were Designed to Cry: So Why Do We Fight Back the Tears?*

[63] Frey, p.31.

[64] The rising rate of heroin addiction is attributed in part to a growing number of young people who started abusing high-end drugs like OxyContin and switched to heroin because it is cheaper and easier to buy. http://www.ncadd.org/index.php/in-the-news/377-prescription-drug-abuse-fueling-rise-in-heroin-addiction.

[65] FROM the CDC's *Morbidity and Mortality Weekly* "Emergency Department Visits Involving Nonmedical Use of Selected Prescription Drugs — United States, 2004—2008," June 18, 2010 / 59(23);705-709, http://www.cdc.gov/mmwr/preview/mmwrhtml/mm5923a1.htm?s_cid=mm5923a1_w.

[66] "Emergency departments see increased visits involving the nonmedical use of sedative alprazolam," *Substance Abuse and Mental Health Services Administration* (SAMHSA), May 22, 2014. http://www.samhsa.gov/newsroom/press-announcements/201405221200.

[67] Ibid.

[68] For more on the possible side effects of antidepressants including the increase in suicidal thoughts visit FDA.gov.

[69] http://www.cbsnews.com/videos/congress-probes-veterans-prescription-drug-overdose-deaths/.

[70] Zondervan, Grand Rapids, MI, 2004, p.19.

[71] Ibid. p.42.

[72] James 1:5-6.

[73] John 10:10.

[74] Isaiah 9:6.

[75] John 16:7,13.

Chapter Seven: *When Tears Won't Come*

[76] Lutz, p.21.

[77] vs.13-16.

[78] Ephesians 3:20.

[79] Isaiah 53:3a.,4a-5.

[80] Acts 10:43.

[81] Scribner, New York, NY, 2005, p.7.

[82] Romans 8:28.

[83] vs.13-14.

[84] vs. 21-22

[85] vs.3,4a-5.

[86] FaithWords, NY, NY, 2012, p.vii.

Chapter Eight: *Crying with Hope: Birthday Reflections from the Graveside*

[87] The term "unpardonable sin" refers to the "blasphemy against the Spirit" spoken about by Jesus in Matthew 12:22-23. Since this term is understood to relate exclusively to the utter rejection of Jesus Christ, it is not possible for a believing Christian to be guilty of this offense. For more information on this subject see *The Billy Graham Christian Worker's Handbook*, edited by Charles G. Ward, World Wide Publications, Charlotte, NC, 2001.

[88] Vine, W.E., *The Expanded Vine's Expository Dictionary of New Testament Words*, ed. by John R. Kohlenberger, III., Bethany House, Minneapolis, MN, 1984, p.563.

[89] Thomas Nelson, Nashville, TN, 1996, p.49.

[90] Romans 6:15 says: *What then? Shall we sin because we are not under law but under grace? By no means!.*

[91] Vine, p.1003.

[92] In John 19:30 Jesus utters the words: "It is finished," or in the Greek, *tetelestai*, a word that was "written on business documents or receipts in New Testament times to indicate that a bill had been paid in full." https://bible.org/question/what-does-greek-word-tetelestai-mean.

[93] Matthew 5:4 (KJV).

Chapter Nine: *Can You Hear Me Now?: How Real Men Can Listen, Learn and Love Through Real Tears*

[94] Morgan Road Books, New York, NY, 2006.

[95] Broadway Books, New York, NY, 2010, pp.96-97.

[96] Ibid.

[97] Jossey-Bass Inc., Publishers, San Francisco, CA, 1996, pp.ix, 124.

[98] Ibid. pp.127,129

[99] Romans 12:2

[100] Frey, p.117

[101] Luke 18:27

[102] 1 Samuel 1:17

Chapter Ten: *The Smallest Yet Greatest Example*

[103] Vine, p.1218.

[104] Ibid.

[105] John 11:25

[106] http://www.gty.org/resources/print/bible-qna/BQ083012

[107] http://www.makotofujimura.com/writings/the-beautiful-tears/. used by permission

[108] http://www.intouch.org/you/bible-studies/content?topic=coping_with_unanswered_prayer_study

[109] Luke 22:41

[110] Mark 14:34

[111] 1 Thessalonians 4:13

[112] *Believer's Bible Commentary*, edited by Art Farstad, Thomas Nelson Publishers, Nashville, TN, 1995, p.1533

[113] A. C. Armstrong & Son, New York, NY, 1890, p.384

Chapter Eleven: *When We Linger*

[114] Used by permission

[115] Romans 8:38

[116] Isaiah 61:3

[117] Romans 5:5

[118] Ephesians 3:20

[119] http://www.crosswalk.com/devotionals/transformgarden/transformation-garden-oct-28-2009-11610367.html

[120] Taken from "Death and the Life After" by Billy Graham, ©1987 Billy Graham. Used by permission

[121] John 16:33

[122] 1 Corinthians 13:8

Chapter Twelve: *After the Flood*

[123] Genesis 9:12-15

[124] Revelation 4:2-3

[125] Revelation 7:17

[126] John 10:18 says: *No one takes it (my life) from me, but I lay it down of my own accord.*

[127] v.6

[128] vs.7-8

In Closing: *A Word for Church Leaders*

[129] Romans 5:4-5

[130] John 6:1-15

[131] Romans 5:5

CONTACT INFORMATION:

Questions and comments concerning this book, as well as requests for speaking engagements with Catherine Cieciuch DeBenedetto, should be sent to:

info@realwomencry.org

For additional information visit:

www.realwomencry.org

Notes

Notes